Parnell

A DOCUMENTARY HISTORY

First published 1991

National Library of Ireland
Kildare Street
Dublin, Ireland.

Tel: (01) 618811
Fax: (01) 766690

ISBN 0 907328 19 9

Front Cover
Parnell in 1881; by Henry O'Shea, a Limerick photographer
(Courtesy of Mrs Ann Fitzgerald)
Prepared for publication by Ms Susan Waine

Back Cover
Avondale
(*Celtic Monthly,* New York, January 1881)

Photographic prints by DM Prints
Typeset by Printset and Design Ltd
Printed by Criterion Press

NOEL KISSANE

Parnell

A DOCUMENTARY HISTORY

NATIONAL LIBRARY OF IRELAND 1991

Foreword

Thomas Carlyle in his book, *On Heroes, Hero-Worship, and the Heroic in History,* has this to say: 'Universal History, the history of what man has accomplished in this world, is at bottom the History of the Great Men who have worked here. They were the leaders of men, these great ones; the modellers, patterns, and in a wide sense creators, of whatsoever the general mass of men contrived to do or to attain...'

Ireland has had many heroes, none more complex or fascinating than Charles Stewart Parnell. Historians use many sources and documents in presenting such historical figures to a contemporary public. The National Library has a great many such sources and this publication brings them together to elucidate and celebrate one of our great statesmen. Many of these documents – manuscripts, drawings, photographs – were donated to the Library, and we acknowledge and pay tribute to the many donors who over the years have added to this incomparable repository.

To Dr Noel Kissane, author of this publication and Education Officer at the National Library, we offer thanks and our congratulations on a job well done.

This publication would not have been possible without the continued enlightened support, both moral and financial, of the Department of the Taoiseach, and this we gratefully acknowledge.

To leave the last word to Carlyle: 'One comfort is, that Great Men, taken up in any way, are profitable company'. We hope you find such company with *Parnell – A Documentary History.*

Dr Pat Donlon, Director,
National Library of Ireland.

A Lawrence photograph of Parnell in 1886.

CONTENTS

Acknowledgements

We are grateful to the following institutions and individuals who have contributed to this publication and an associated exhibition by kindly permitting us to reproduce documents in their custody or by providing items for display:

Ms Eileen Brereton; Coillte Teoranta; Dublin Civic Museum; Dublin Diocesan Archives and Most Rev. Dr Desmond Connell, D.D., Archbishop of Dublin; Mrs Ann Fitzgerald; Rev. Christopher Halliday, Rector, St Saviour's Church, Rathdrum; The Hugh Lane Municipal Gallery of Modern Art; Mrs Nuala Jordan; Kilmainham Jail; Mayo County Library; The National Archives; The National Gallery of Ireland; The National Museum of Ireland; Office of Public Works; The Parnell Society; The Registry of Deeds; Ms Máire Tobin; The Board Of Trinity College, Dublin; Wicklow County Library.

The staff in various institutions were extremely generous with their time and facilities, and the guidance and advice which they provided on sources for the study of Parnell were invaluable; the following deserve special recognition: Mr Paul Byrne, Secretary, Coillte Teoranta; Mr Aodh Ó Tuama, Curator, Cork Public Museum; Mr Tom O'Connor, Curator, Dublin Civic Museum; Mr David Sheehy, Archivist, Dublin Diocesan Archives; Ms Liz Turley, Acting Director, and Ms Patricia Flavin, Hugh Lane Municipal Gallery; Ms Majella McLoughlin, Kilmainham Jail; Mr Pat McMahon, County Librarian, Mayo County Library; Dr David Craig, Director, and Dr Philomena Connolly, Mr Ken Hannigan and Ms Aideen Ireland, National Archives; Mr Bill Bolger, Head of Visual Communications, National College of Art and Design; Mr Adrian Le Harivel, Ms Paula Hicks and Ms Ann Stewart, National Gallery; Dr Patrick F. Wallace, Director, Mr John Teahan, Keeper, and Mr Michael Kenny, National Museum; Mr Con Brogan, Photographer, Office of Public Works; Mr Charles Benson, Keeper, and Mr Vincent Kinane, Trinity College Library; Mr Joseph Hayes, County Librarian, Wicklow County Library.

The following individuals were particularly helpful and are most gratefully acknowledged: Mr Harry Bradshaw, Mr Edward Chandler, Mr Dermot Collery, Ms Mary Davies (for the map of Avondale on page 10), Ms Ann Cuffe Fitzgerald, Professor Roy Foster, Mr Dáithí Hanly, Mr Kieran Hickey (for drawing attention to a number of important documents), Mr Harry Latham, the late Professor F.S.L. Lyons, Dr J.B. Lyons, Professor R.B. McDowell, Dr Edward McParland, Ms Dymphna Moore, Dr Conor O'Brien, Professor Maurice O'Connell, Mr Seán Ó Mórdha, Professor T.P. O'Neill, Mrs Nora O'Shea, Mr Glenn Thompson, Dr Kevin Whelan. Mr Frank Callanan kindly read the text and made a number of valuable suggestions. We are particularly grateful to Mr John Farrell of the National Museum who mounted the exhibition. The staff of Criterion Press and of Printset and Design, especially Ms Maureen Gallagher, Mr Tom Fay and Mr John Gibney, have been most helpful and efficient in getting the book into print.

Finally, several colleagues in the National Library have assisted with the book or the exhibition; those who were most often called upon were: Mr Donal F. Begley, Chief Herald of Ireland, Mr Kevin Browne, Mr Tom Desmond, Mr Gerard Long, Ms Sinéad Looby, Mr Gerard Lyne, Mr John Lyons, Mr Philip McCann, Dr Éilís Ní Dhuibhne and Mr Dónall Ó Luanaigh. In addition two members of staff merit special acknowledgement and gratitude: Ms Marie O'Gallagher who typed the manuscript with speed and precision; and Mr Eugene Hogan, the National Library's photographer, who produced a considerable number of high quality photographs for the book and the exhibition.

Editorial note

Most of the documents are given in the form of transcripts. They are reproduced verbatim but many are abbreviated. Each transcript begins with a heading (in bold type) which is taken from the document itself – for instance, an extract from a book usually has the chapter heading or sub-heading. Each transcript ends with the source reference, generally in abbreviated form.

The punctuation of the transcripts is to some extent standardised in accordance with current practice. To preserve the spirit of the originals, however, some archaic styles are retained; for example, capital letters used to indicate emphasis have not been reduced to lower case in instances where they seem especially significant.

Editorial comment is kept to the minimum and its only function is to set the context for the documents. The evidence presented by many of the documents could, of course, be disputed, since writers, reporters or artists may not always be accurate or honest. Readers must make their own judgements, and for each a different Parnell may emerge.

Introduction

As one of the most controversial political figures of his day, Charles Stewart Parnell was the subject of a great deal of contemporary documentation. Much of this survives in the form of newspaper reports, official publications, pamphlets and posters. There were also the more personal manuscript documents, including letters, diaries, memoranda and other scripts penned by such diverse players in the Parnell drama as his mistress Katharine O'Shea, the forger Richard Pigott, Archbishop Croke of Cashel, and the 'Uncrowned King' himself. Most of this historical source material is preserved in libraries and archives, at home and abroad, and is usually seen only by academics and other serious students of Irish history. The ordinary person may, of course, benefit from the original documentation indirectly, by reading the books and articles published by the scholars, but has to be content with their interpretations, enlivened, perhaps, by occasional quotations or illustrations.

This publication is an attempt at making an interesting cross-section of the source material readily available to the general reader. It is designed as a documentary history of Parnell and is intended to bring the reader into more intimate contact with the man and his times than is the case with the normal biography. It should also help to make people more aware of the nature of historical sources and of the evidence upon which historians base their theories and assessments.

For political personalities of the nineteenth century the newspapers of the period are one of the most important and accessible sources of information. In the case of Parnell, all the important incidents of his career, from his unsuccessful campaign for a parliamentary seat for Co. Dublin in 1874 to his death in 1891, were reported in the national press. The factual reporting, for instance regarding the content of speeches, was generally accurate, but naturally the editorial comment of such politically committed newspapers as the *Freeman's Journal* or the *Irish Times* has to be regarded with caution. The same is the case with the provincial papers. For instance, in 1875 the *Drogheda Argus* was a most enthusiastic supporter of Parnell's candidature for Co. Meath, whereas throughout his political career his local *Wicklow Newsletter* regarded him as one who, sadly, had turned his back on his own class and creed.

The most important decade of Parnell's career, that of the eighties, coincided with the publication of regular weekly colour supplements to some of the newspapers. Generally, they took the form of political cartoons, and the artists of the *Weekly Freeman* and the *Weekly Irish Times* vied with each other in producing topical and arresting commentary on the issues of the day. A notable contributor in that genre was Parnell's own newspaper, *United Ireland,* the cartoonist of which, J.D. Reigh, was complimented by Parnell as 'the only one who can do justice to my handsome face'.

As one of the major figures on the Westminster stage, Parnell also featured prominently in the British press. In particular, two very influential weekly magazines, the *Illustrated London News* and *The Graphic,* represented many of the important Parnell stories in evocative engravings. For instance, the central figures and the more dramatic scenes from the Special Commission hearings of 1888-89 were sketched on the spot by Sydney Prior Hall and published in *The Graphic.* Many of Hall's original drawings and his posthumous painting of Parnell are now in the National Gallery of Ireland.

In parliament, Parnell obviously made a major contribution, both in debate and in the corpus of legislation for which he was the catalyst, and his input can be researched in the official publications of the period. His speeches in parliament are reported verbatim in Hansard's *Parliamentary Debates,* and the various bills and acts with which he was involved are also available in print. Another important official source is the published record of the proceedings of the Special Commission where, in effect, Parnell was on trial and obliged to make a detailed public defence of his political career. This massive work amounts to twelve volumes and Parnell's evidence runs to 400 pages.

Parnell's public career is well documented, but by nature he was secretive and reticent, and it is difficult to get detailed and incontrovertible information on his personality and private life. However, there are a number of interesting reminiscences, memoirs and biographies by various colleagues in the Irish Parliamentary Party, including Justin McCarthy, William O'Brien and T.P. O'Connor, all of whom were journalists who had friendly personal relationships with him for many years. The first well-researched biography, *The Life of Charles Stewart Parnell,* was published in 1898 by Richard Barry O'Brien, who also was a journalist and knew him well for almost a decade. In addition, Parnell featured very prominently in books by three other people with whom he was even more closely involved – his sister Emily (Mrs Dickinson), his brother, John Howard, and Katharine O'Shea. The least satisfactory is that of Emily which, in many passages, is recklessly fanciful. John Howard's memoir is a relatively reliable work which gives an informed and balanced account of many otherwise un-documented aspects of Parnell from his childhood to his latter years. Finally, Katharine O'Shea's book is the only source for the domestic life which Parnell shared with her at Eltham and it includes a number of unique photographs. The work runs to two volumes and altogether is a fascinating record of a most intriguing love affair.

Manuscript documents are by their nature unique and in the case of a historical figure such as Parnell they tend to be less accessible than the printed sources. Generally, they are dispersed among a variety of archives and libraries, and individual items have to be traced through catalogues and indexes. Parnell's own private manuscript papers have not survived, but there are small collections of his letters and other items in a number of repositories. Also, the papers of some of his close associates are preserved in various libraries. For instance, the papers of John Dillon and Michael Davitt are in the Library of Trinity College, Dublin, and those of William O'Brien are split between University College, Cork, and the National Library. The National Library also has the papers of a number of other colleagues of Parnell, including Isaac Butt, T.C. Harrington and John Redmond. All of these collections are important sources for the study of Parnell, the Irish Parliamentary Party and the period.

In addition to the manuscripts of individuals, there are also the files accumulated at the time by various organisations, for instance the administration in Dublin Castle and the Catholic hierarchy. The reports on Parnell and other activists, which were forwarded to Dublin Castle by the local constabulary during the Land League agitation, are available for consultation in the National Archives. Similarly, some of the bishops with whom Parnell had dealings preserved their correspondence as a matter of routine, and there is considerable material in a number of diocesan archives, most notably those of Dublin and Cashel.

Elsewhere in Ireland there are important collections of Parnell memorabilia in institutions such as the National Museum, Kilmainham Jail and, of course, Avondale. Also, there are many manuscript documents still in private custody, but as time goes on more and more of them are being deposited in libraries and archives. In addition, many of the letters and manuscripts written by Parnell himself are located among the papers of the various people abroad with whom he corresponded. Most of these are in Britain, in collections such as the Gladstone Papers in the British Library and the Chamberlain Papers in Birmingham University Library. Apart from including actual Parnell documents, the papers of many of the prominent British politicians of the period contain a great deal of material that is of primary importance for a proper understanding of various critical aspects of the Parnell story.

This selection of documents includes extracts or illustrations from most of the sources referred to above. The aim is to introduce the reader to original sources, to give some impression of their nature and variety, and to promote an interest in history and in the writing of history. Ultimately, one would hope that some readers may be stimulated into undertaking actual historical research on Parnell or some other subject. In the case of Parnell, the literature is already extensive but by no means exhaustive. No doubt, as research continues and as new evidence comes to light, the man and his personality will continue to come into sharper focus. However, Parnell was a most complicated phenomenon and will always, no doubt, to some extent remain an enigma and a challenge for historians.

The Sources

1. Books and pamphlets

A Cambridge Scrap-book (London, 1859).

Michael Davitt, *Leaves from a Prison Diary* (London, 1885).

Michael Davitt, *The Fall of Feudalism in Ireland* (London and New York, 1904).

Devoy's Postbag, ed. by William O'Brien and D. Ryan (2 vols., Dublin, 1948, 1953).

Emily Dickinson, *A Patriot's Mistake: Reminiscences of the Parnell Family, by a Daughter of the House* (London, 1905).

Roy Foster, *Charles Stewart Parnell: the Man and His Family* (Hassocks, Sussex, 1976).

T.M. Healy, *Letters and Leaders of My Day* (2 vols. London, 1929).

James Joyce, *Ulysses* (Odyssey Press, Hamburg, 1932).

Justin McCarthy, *Reminiscences* (Dublin, 1891).

R.B. O'Brien, *Life of Charles Stewart Parnell* (2 vols., London, 1898).

William O'Brien, *The Parnell of Real Life* (London, 1926).

T.P. O'Connor, *Charles Stewart Parnell, a Memory* (London, 1891).

T.P. O'Connor, *Memories of an Old Parliamentarian* (2 vols., London, 1929).

Katharine O'Shea, *Charles Stewart Parnell: His Love Story and Political Life* (2 vols., London, 1914).

Parliamentary Debates, ed. T.C. Hansard (London, vols. 1875, 1876, 1887).

Charles Stewart Parnell (*Daily Graphic* Pamphlets I, London, 1890).

Mr. Parnell as a Landlord and a "Land-Grabber" [Dublin, *c.* 1885].

Sir Henry Brooke Parnell, *A History of the Penal Laws against the Irish Catholics from the Treaty of Limerick to the Union* (Dublin, 1808).

John Howard Parnell, *Charles Stewart Parnell: A Memoir* (London, 1916).

[William Parnell-Hayes], *An Enquiry into the Causes of Popular Discontents in Ireland by an Irish Country Gentleman* (Dublin, 1804).

The Parnell Commission [London, 1890].

Report of the Special Commission, 1888 (London, 1890).

Special Commission Act 1888, Minutes of Evidence (12 vols., London, 1890).

Thoms's County Directory (Dublin, 1875).

W.B. Yeats, 'Come Gather Round Me Parnellites', in *A Cuala Press Broadside* (Dublin, January 1937).

2. Newspapers and Magazines

Celtic Magazine (New York)

Celtic Monthly (New York)

Connaught Telegraph (Castlebar)

Daily Graphic (London)

Daily Sketch (London)

Drogheda Argus

Evening News and Post (London)

Freeman's Journal (Dublin)

The Graphic (London)

Illustrated London News

Irish Times (Dublin)

Irish World (New York)

Le Monde Illustré (Paris)

The Nation (Dublin)

National Press (Dublin)

Pall Mall Gazette (London)

The Times (London)

The Union (Dublin)

United Ireland (Dublin)

Weekly Freeman (Dublin)

Weekly News (Dublin)

Wicklow Newsletter and General Advertiser

3. Manuscripts

Dublin Diocesan Archives

Archbishop Walsh Papers (Pigott to Walsh; Croke to Walsh; Brownrigg to Walsh).

National Archives

CSO/RP/1881/40,461 (Dr Kenny's Journal).

National Library of Ireland (NLI)

MS 4572 (re chairmanship of Irish party).

MS 5385 (re Captain O'Shea, February 1886).

MS 5934 (Parnell to Lord Howth; re Parnell's marriage).

MS 10,514 (proposal to set up a newspaper).

MS 13,504 (re divorce).

MS 13,506 (Parnell to T.P. Gill; Parnell to William O'Brien, 1890).

MS 13,507 (Parnell to William O'Brien, 1891).

MS 18,041 (Irish Famine Relief Fund).

MS 21,933 (manifesto, 1890).

Registry of Deeds

Memorial, 1869, 27.67 (Avondale estate).

St Saviour's Church, Rathdrum

Parish Register, 1846 (Parnell's baptism).

4. Illustrations

Avondale (Parnell at House of Commons).

Dublin Civic Museum (State trials).

Mrs Ann Fitzgerald (Parnell in 1881).

Kilmainham Jail (John Henry Parnell; Clare and Katharine O'Shea).

National Library of Ireland: Most of the illustrations are from books or newspapers in the National Library; also a number of items are from the National Library's Collection of Prints and Drawings (**NLI P&D**).

Trinity College Library (The Irish Parliamentary Party, 1886).

CHAPTER I

Formation

The Parnells of Avondale, Co. Wicklow, were descended from an English merchant family which came to prominence in the town of Congleton in Cheshire early in the seventeenth century. Those Parnells were active in local politics, a father and son both held the office of mayor of Congleton, and during the Civil War they supported the Parliament. The Irish branch of the family was established soon after the restoration of Charles II in 1660, when Thomas Parnell purchased an estate at Rathleague in Queen's County, now Co. Laois. Over the years the Irish Parnells produced a fair quota of notable personalities including, in the first generation, the poet Thomas Parnell, who was well known in his day. Better known to posterity was Sir John Parnell who became Chancellor of the Exchequer in Grattan's Parliament. He lost office in 1799 when he opposed the Act of Union, a move motivated more by self-interest than patriotism.

The Avondale estate came into the family through Sir John who inherited it from his cousin and political ally Samuel Hayes, MP. One of Sir John's elder sons, Henry Brooke Parnell, succeeded to the baronetcy, but Avondale passed to a younger son, William, grandfather of Charles Stewart. In tribute to Samuel Hayes, William adopted the surname Parnell-Hayes, but this style was not continued in the following generation. In politics, William and Henry Brooke were more progressive than their father and were concerned with the plight of the rural poor. Though Protestants themselves, they were also concerned with the disabilities of Roman Catholics. They championed reform in both these areas, as members of the United Kingdom parliament and in a number of published works.

On William's death in 1821, his son John Henry inherited Avondale and, providentially it would seem, much of his humane and liberal outlook. However, John Henry, father of Charles Stewart, played little part in politics and was the first in his line for five generations who did not become an MP. Instead, he concentrated on managing and improving his estate. But he also held some of the public offices appropriate to a man of his class; for instance, he was chairman of the Rathdrum Poor Law Union, and Deputy Lieutenant and High Sheriff for Co. Wicklow.

During a tour of the United States with his cousin, Lord Powerscourt, John Henry visited Washington where he met a society belle, Delia Tudor Stewart. The couple married in 1835 and settled down at Avondale. They had twelve children, all of whom were born by 1853. Thereafter, they seem to have lived mostly apart. John Henry and some of the children continued on at Avondale while Delia and the remainder spent much of the time in Paris with her mother and brother.

Due to the virtual separation of the parents, the children's upbringing was rather unorthodox and their education was episodic. In addition, in 1859, when Charles Stewart was thirteen, John Henry died suddenly leaving his affairs in disorder. Under the terms of the will, the brothers John Howard and Henry Tudor got estates in Co. Armagh and Co. Carlow, and Charles Stewart, contrary to his expectations, inherited Avondale. As minors, the children were made wards of court, Avondale was rented out and the family went to live in Dublin.

Ancestors

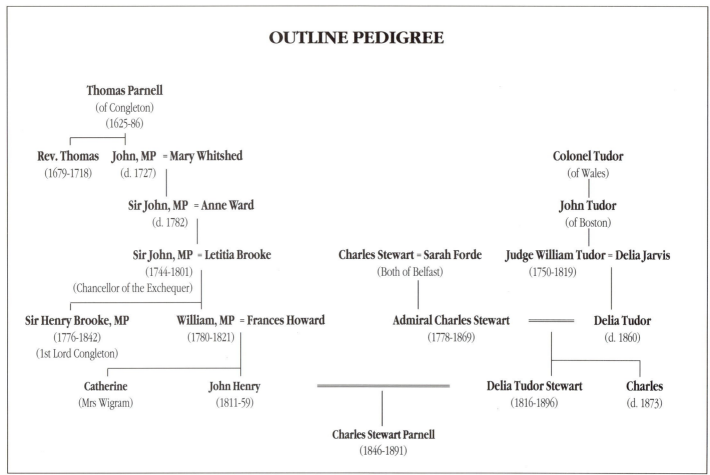

OUTLINE PEDIGREE

Thomas Parnell
(of Congleton)
(1625-86)

Rev. Thomas — John, MP = Mary Whitshed
(1679-1718)   (d. 1727)

Colonel Tudor
(of Wales)

Sir John, MP = Anne Ward
(d. 1782)

John Tudor
(of Boston)

Sir John, MP = Letitia Brooke
(1744-1801)
(Chancellor of the Exchequer)

Charles Stewart = Sarah Forde
(Both of Belfast)

Judge William Tudor = Delia Jarvis
(1750-1819)

Sir Henry Brooke, MP   William, MP = Frances Howard
(1776-1842)   (1780-1821)
(1st Lord Congleton)

Admiral Charles Stewart
(1778-1869)

Delia Tudor
(d. 1860)

Catherine   John Henry
(Mrs Wigram)   (1811-59)

Delia Tudor Stewart   Charles
(1816-1896)   (d. 1873)

Charles Stewart Parnell
(1846-1891)

Thomas Parnell, Archdeacon of Clogher, poet
and friend of Swift and Pope. (NLI P&D)

The Right Hon.ble
Sir JOHN PARNELL Bart.
Knight of the Shire for the Queens County &
late Chancellor of the Exchequer in Ireland

Admiral Charles Stewart; in 1812, during the war between America and England, he captured two British ships and was afterwards called 'Old Ironsides.' (*Celtic Magazine*, September 1882)

A
HISTORY
OF THE
PENAL LAWS
AGAINST THE
IRISH CATHOLICS
FROM
THE TREATY OF LIMERICK TO THE UNION
By HENRY PARNELL, Esq M. P.

Title of a work by Sir Henry Brooke Parnell, MP (Dublin, 1808) .

AN
INQUIRY
INTO
THE CAUSES
OF
POPULAR DISCONTENTS
IN
IRELAND
BY
AN IRISH COUNTRY GENTLEMAN

Title of a work by William Parnell-Hayes, MP (Dublin, 1804).

Below: Grattan's Parliament, 1790. Parnell often referred in idealistic terms to Grattan's Parliament of 1782-1800 in which his great- grandfather, Sir John Parnell (arrowed), was Chancellor of the Exchequer. (NLI P&D)

Childhood

Charles Stewart Parnell was born at Avondale where he grew up as one of a large family. Between the ages of six and nineteen he attended a total of five schools in England. The first was at Yeovil in Somerset which he left after he contracted typhoid. From the time he was seven until his father's death when he was thirteen his mother spent much of her time in Paris.

His father, John Henry Parnell, as a child. (Kilmainham Jail)

His mother, Delia Tudor Stewart Parnell. She was the daughter of Admiral Stewart, and a grand-daughter of Judge William Tudor, a distinguished soldier of the American Revolution and a legislator for Massachusetts. (E. Dickinson, *A Patriot's Mistake*)

Charles Stewart Parnell at eight years of age. (E. Dickinson, *A Patriot's Mistake*)

THE CHILDREN

Name	Date of Birth	Date of Death
William	1837	1842
Delia; married J.L. Thomson	1838	1882
Hayes	1839	1854
Emily; married (1) Captain Dickinson, (2) Captain Ricketts	1841	1918
John Howard; married Mrs Mateer	1843	1923
Sophia; married Alfred McDermott	1845	1877
CHARLES STEWART; married Mrs O'Shea	27 June 1846	6 October 1891
Fanny	1849	1882
Henry Tudor; married Penelope Luby	1850	1915
Anna Katherine	1852	1911
Theodosia; married Captain Paget	1853	1920

Also, one child, a boy, stillborn

(Compiled from J.H. Parnell, *C.S. Parnell*, p.11; and Roy Foster, *Parnell*, p. 65)

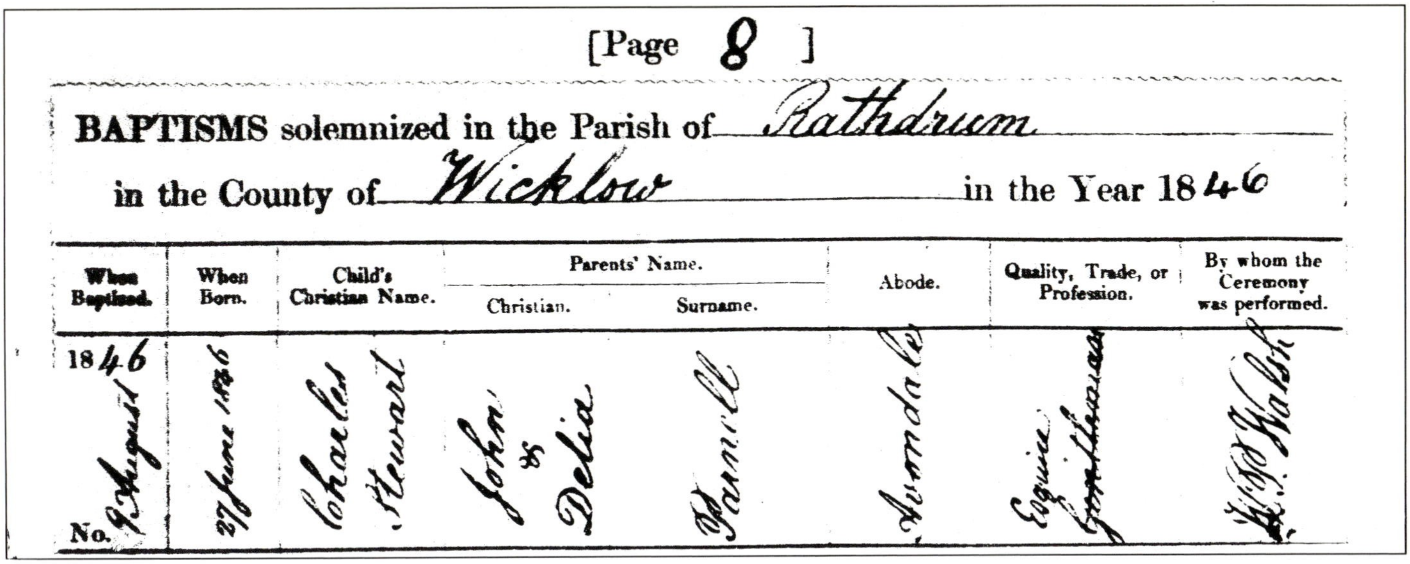

[Page 8]

BAPTISMS solemnized in the Parish of Rathdrum
in the County of Wicklow in the Year 1846

When Baptised.	When Born.	Child's Christian Name.	Parents' Name. Christian.	Parents' Name. Surname.	Abode.	Quality, Trade, or Profession.	By whom the Ceremony was performed.
1846 9 August No.	27 June 1846	Charles Stewart	John & Delia	Parnell	Avondale	Esquire Gentleman	[illegible] Walsh

An extract from the parish register at St Saviour's Church, Rathdrum, recording that Charles Stewart Parnell was baptised on 9 August 1846. He was named Charles Stewart after his uncle and grandfather.

Note: The first transcript documents:

Child-life at Avondale

In a large family the different members often divide in twos and twos, each one having his own special 'chum'. Thus Hayes and I were chums, John and Katherine [i.e. Anna], whilst the latest arrival, baby Fanny, fell to the share of Charles who, from an early age, exhibited a masterful propensity for dictating to and managing others, assuming the leadership, and trying to set the world and its pilgrims right. In order to get his own way with his brothers and sisters, he would 'butt' us all round with his head, like a goat, so that he acquired the name amongst us of 'Butt-head'. His high spirits, which would not brook control, proved a source of great trouble to his nurses and later on to his governesses and tutors who, one and all, found themselves incapable of managing him, though a word of tender remonstrance from his mother would appeal at once to his affectionate disposition and curb his most turbulent outbreaks of passionate temper.

(E. Dickinson, *A Patriot's Mistake,* pp. 8-9)

Home Tuition

After leaving school [at Yeovil] he was taught by our sisters' governess. He was then eight years old and more strongly than ever resented being taught by a woman, and so constantly did he protest that our parents judged it wiser to get him a tutor. From this time forward, he seemed to take a greater interest in his lessons but, in spite of this, he was by no means an easy pupil to teach. His ambition (marked even in those days) was never satisfied, and he always wanted to be with bigger boys. Consequently, the arguments between tutor and pupil were many and fierce, and in the long-run, if the truth be told, it was the boy who generally proved the victor. Nor was the effort to give him religious instruction attended with any better success. When he was not in the mood to listen, he turned everything into ridicule and sent his instructor away hopelessly saddened.This high-spirited boy gave his confidence to very few, but, once given, it was deep and true and lasting. As he grew in later years, he rapidly became more and more reserved. He had all the healthy boy's love of games, especially cricket, which he already played well in those early years. Even then he loved to lead in games, as he did subsequently in politics.

(J.H. Parnell, *C.S. Parnell*, pp. 28-29)

Adolescence

John Henry Parnell died in 1859. In his will he made suitable provision for his eldest son, John Howard, but he left Avondale to Charles Stewart. As minors the children were then made wards of court. Until Charles Stewart came of age, Avondale was rented out and the family found other accommodation.

For most of the 1860s, while the children were wards in Chancery, the family lived away from Avondale, first at Khyber Pass in Dalkey, then in Kingstown (Dun Laoghaire), and finally for several years in Temple Street in Dublin. From 1862 to 1865 Charles Stewart and his brother, John Howard, attended a private school run by the Rev. Alexander Wishaw at Chipping Norton in Oxfordshire.

As heir to Avondale, Charles spent the holidays there and had a great interest in the estate, the tenants and the rural life of Co. Wicklow. In his late teens he joined the local militia, the Wicklow Rifles, as was customary for spirited young men of the landlord class. He was promoted to lieutenant on 25 February 1865 and retired in 1870.

A Great Bereavement

Charley was at this time (1859) about thirteen and living at Avondale with our father, while I was at school in Paris with Monsieur Roderon, learning French, drawing, and a little painting. My sisters were also in school at Paris. Our uncle, Charles Stewart, of 'Ironsides', Bordentown, USA, the son of Commodore Charles Stewart, our mother's father, was living in 51 Champs Elysées, with his mother, Mrs Stewart. Our married sister, Mrs Thomson, was also in Paris, living in the Faubourg St-Germain. We were all very happy, when a telegram arrived to say that our father had died suddenly at the Shelbourne Hotel, Dublin. He was always an enthusiastic cricketer, and had gone up to Dublin to play in a big match between the Leinster and the Phoenix teams, although for some time he had been under the doctor's care, suffering from rheumatism of the stomach, and had been warned by Sir Frederick March not to indulge in violent exercise. But he had a determined will and, like Charley, when he had made up his mind to a thing, carried it out at all cost. The result was that, although in a high fever, he insisted on playing in the match. He felt worse on his return to the hotel and sent for a doctor; but it was too late, and he died next day. His death came as a thunderbolt to us all, as he was always regarded as the healthiest of the whole family.

He was buried quietly at Mount Jerome, my brother Charley being the only member of the family to see him laid at rest, as all the others were abroad. After the funeral, my mother, my sisters, and myself, returned to Dublin, where we stopped in lodgings near Gardiner Street.

It was here that our father's will was read. Avondale was left to Charley; the Armagh estate (Collure) to myself; and the Carlow property to Henry. I well remember Charley standing by our mother's bed discussing our father's will, and saying, 'I suppose John has got Avondale', and when mother told him it was his, he was greatly surprised and said he never expected it.

Wards in Chancery

After this, our mother took steps to have us all made wards in Chancery after consulting the guardians, Sir Ralph Howard, Bart., and Mr Johnson. Sir Ralph Howard was annoyed at being joint guardian with Mr Johnson, who was a Scotch agricultural expert, and an old friend of our father's.

Once we were made wards in Chancery, Mr McDermott (our father's solicitor), who managed our affairs under the direction of the Court of Chancery, arranged to have us placed in our mother's charge and we all went down to Avondale. It was a sad home-coming for the young heir, my brother Charley. Mr McDermott came down to take charge of father's affairs and to go through the papers. He found everything in a very confused state, and his first act was to pay off all the workmen not actually required; while, by order of the Court, the live-stock and farming implements were sold by auction. Sufficient horses for the use of the family were kept, and the rest sold. Mr West, of Mount Avon, was appointed agent. The servants were kept on, and one of them, indeed – a faithful old retainer named Martin Walsh – would have refused to leave us under any circumstances. Miss Zouche, a devoted relative, who had been acting as house-keeper, remained at Avondale for a year to take charge of the house while our affairs were being put in order.

We then moved to Dalkey, about eight miles from Dublin, along the sea-coast, the Court deciding on a house named Khyber Pass as being a suitable residence for us. This house was situated on a very high hill, overlooking the sea and the railway, and I remember clearly the beautiful view we had of the sea in the distance.

Charley was now more of a companion for me, and he and I spent most of our time together. My sisters had a governess, and Charley and I a tutor. When our studies were over, he and I used to go out together.

Nearing Manhood

At the time of Charley's return [from Chipping Norton] our mother was keeping open house in Temple Street, giving dinners, balls, and small dances, to her many Dublin friends. Charley

Parnell in his Wicklow Rifles uniform. The uniform was dark green with black facings (collar and cuffs). His right hand is on his shako (head-dress). (T.M. Healy, *Letters*, vol.i)

was very popular in society, going to all the dances and parties. He used to admire and, dance with all the pretty girls at the balls given by Lord Carlisle, then Lord Lieutenant of Ireland.

Charley soon decided to join the militia. One trivial reason that influenced him was that by doing so he would be able to wear uniform at the Castle, as he particularly disliked the levee dress, declaring it looked too much like a footman's livery. He found that there were vacancies in the Wicklow Rifles and also in the Armagh Light Infantry; but, as he was a Wicklow landed proprietor, he chose the former, while, as my estate was in Armagh, I joined the Armagh Light Infantry. We had some training at the Royal Barracks in Dublin before joining our respective regiments, which were also afterwards called out for training. Charley told me that he had a very enjoyable time when training with his regiment, as he went to no end of dinners, dances, and garden parties, and I, too, had very much the same experience with the Armaghs. While we were in the militia, Charley and I attended all the levees, and drawing-rooms, and other entertainments at Dublin Castle. The Lord Lieutenant, Lord Carlisle, being a friend of our mother's, used to talk to us a good deal, especially about our cricket matches.

(J.H. Parnell, *C.S. Parnell*, pp. 38-41, 54-5)

Cambridge

When he was nineteen Parnell entered Magdalene College, Cambridge. However, he did not apply himself to study and left without a degree after almost four years. In 1867, while he was still at Cambridge, he came of age and assumed control of the estate at Avondale. He adopted it as his residence but only spent the holidays there until he left Cambridge.

Cambridge, as it looked in Parnell's time. (*A Cambridge Scrap-book*, 1858)

At College

Shortly after our return from Chipping Norton, Charley went up to Cambridge, but I did not accompany him. He was at Cambridge from 1865 to 1869, but spent little time there and left owing to his getting into serious trouble. I understood afterwards that an action for assault was successfully brought against him in the Cambridge County Court by a merchant named Hamilton, twenty guineas damages being awarded. The evidence in court was of a conflicting nature, and Charley never told me his version of the affair. His references to his undergraduate days were very brief and reserved, though he appeared to have got on badly with the other fellows, and to have had many quarrels which often resulted in blows. On one occasion, he told me afterwards, five students came to his bedroom for what would now be called a 'rag', and after a desperate struggle he succeeded in throwing them all out.

In any event, the college authorities decided to send him down for the remainder of the term, of which, however, there was only a fortnight left. Although there was no reason why he should not have returned at the beginning of the next term as he had not been expelled, he steadily refused to do so, and his education thus concluded without his taking a degree.

There is no doubt that the fact of his never having been at a real school, and having a continual change of tutors, coupled with the perfunctory nature of his studies at college, considerably hampered him in after-life. He often expressed to me his regret that he had not devoted himself with more application to such opportunities as he had for study. One result was that he was always afraid of lapsing into an error of grammar or spelling, and for a considerable time wrote out his speeches word for word and carefully corrected them before delivery. His letters, also, throughout his career show frequent signs of erasure and alteration.

(J.H. Parnell, *C.S. Parnell*, pp. 52-53)

Rejoicing

The coming of age of Charles Stewart Parnell, Esq., of Avondale in the county, was celebrated with great rejoicing and festivity at the family residence at Avondale on Thursday the 27th instant by the tenantry, retainers and work-people of the property.

Mr Parnell, who is deservedly popular amongst all those with whom he is in any way connected, was unavoidably absent on the occasion, important business in the Court of Chancery, in which he was a ward during his minority, having required his presence before the Lord Chancellor. But a plentiful and sumptuous entertainment was provided by his orders for all those who are in any way connected with the estate and, in fact it might be said, for all comers, and we need scarcely say that Mr Parnell's hospitality was largely availed of.

The rejoicing was opened with large bonfires which were kept ablaze for a considerable time and were regarded as signals for a regular gathering of the merry-makers of the neighbourhood. Many were the jokes and long was the laughter which mingled with the crackling of the faggots of the joy-fires, and frequent and hearty were the wishes expressed for the health and happiness of the worthy young squire.

After the company had partaken of the good cheer provided for them, the health of Mr Parnell was proposed in a speech well suited for the occasion by Mr John Kavanagh of Ballyknockan, one of the tenants of the estate, and seconded in a short but appropriate manner by Mr Laurence McGrath. The toast was received with the greatest manifestations of goodwill, and three times three given for Mr Parnell with a heartiness and a cordiality which were infinitely creditable alike to that gentleman,

Parnell at twenty years of age. (E. Dickinson, *A Patriot's Mistake*)

and his tenantry, and people. Dancing and feasting were kept up till an advanced hour in the morning, when all parties quietly returned to their homes highly delighted with their entertainment.

It is with feelings of great pleasure that we give publicity to the above narrative of festivity and rejoicing, which we fully believe were neither more nor less than the occasion required. Mr Parnell is a young gentleman of no ordinary talent and capacity, and we hope ere long to see him assume that position in his native county which his own talents and station, as well as his ancestral antecedents, so fully entitle him.

(*Wicklow Newsletter*, 29 June 1867)

Squire of Avondale

In the early 1870s Parnell concentrated on managing and improving his estate. He was particularly interested in exploiting the extensive forestry on the property and operated a sawmill on the Avonmore River. He had a good relationship with the tenants and was generally concerned for their welfare.

His annual income from Avondale, from farms in Co. Carlow and houses in Dublin, amounted to over £2,000. However, he had debts of £18,500 on which he paid £1,100 a year interest. In addition, he paid annuities of £100 each to his sisters Emily and Delia, and he had to support various members of the family when they were at Avondale.

Parnell was very conscious of the civic responsibilities of the landed gentry and while still in his twenties he took on various public duties. He became a magistrate, a Grand Juror in the Wicklow Assizes and represented his diocese in the Synod of the Church of Ireland. In 1874 he became High Sheriff for the county, a largely honorary post once held by his father which involved acting as returning officer at elections and empanelling the Grand Jury.

THE AVONDALE ESTATE

Lands	Division	Gross Yearly Rents
		£ s d
Avondale	Ballytrasna	260 0 0
Casino	”	94 10 0
Ballytrasna	”	237 15 10
(Ballyknockan)	”	
Kingston		225 5 11
”	”	301 13 0
The Meetings	”	124 13 10
Tyclash	”	36 11 9
Ballyteague	”	16 10 0
Ballyeustace	”	65 0 0
Garrymore	Glenmalure	42 18 4
Clonkeen	”	
Caravellagh	”	
(Corasillagh)	”	63 15 0
Bomaskea	”	57 18 0
Carrignamuck	Aughavannagh	74 4 0
Carrignaweel	”	75 15 0
Aughavannagh	”	80 0 0
Coraskilla and Branskey mines	”	40 0 0

3807 acres	£1,789 10 11

In addition to the rents listed he made an additional £280 a year from other rents from the property. (Registry of Deeds, Memorial 1869, 27.67)

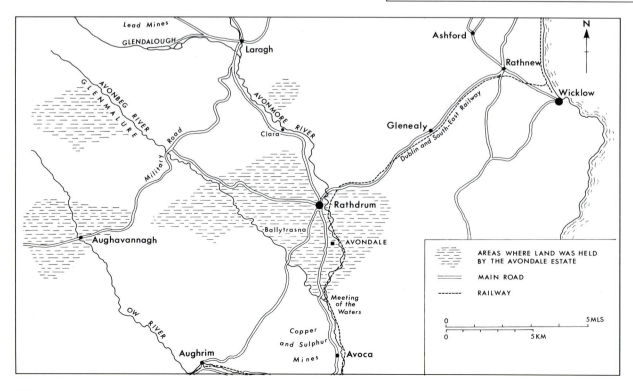

10

Her Majesty's Lieutenant of the County and Custos Rotulorum.

Right Hon. the Earl of MEATH (1869), *Colonel of the County Dublin Militia* (J.P. and D.L. co. Dublin; was M.P. for co. Dublin, 1830–33, 1837–41), Kilruddery Castle, Bray; Travellers' Club, London, S.W.

High Sheriff (1874-75).

CHARLES STEWART PARNELL, esq. (J.P. co. Wicklow), Avondale, Rathdrum.

Members of Parliament for the County.

WILLIAM RICHARD O'BYRNE, esq. (1874), (J.P. for cos. Wicklow and Dublin), Cabinteely House, co. Dublin; Glenealy, co. Wicklow; Grove Lodge, Hayes, Middlesex; Athenæum Club, London, S.W.

WILLIAM WENTWORTH FITZWILLIAM DICK, esq. (1852), D.L., Humewood, Kiltegan, in this county; 20, Curzon-street, May Fair, London, W.; Carlton Club, London, S.W.

Deputy Lieutenants.

Deputy Lieutenants and Magistrates marked thus (*) have served the office of High Sheriff in this County.

Aldborough, Right Hon. the Earl of (late Capt. 1st Dr. Gds.), Stratford Lodge, Baltinglass; Junior United Service Club, London, S.W.

*Bayly, Lieut.-Col. Edward Symes (late Lieut.-Col. Wicklow Militia, and formerly Captain 34th Foot), Ballyarthur, Ovoca; Kildare-street Club, Dublin

*Carroll, Henry, Ballynure, Grange, Athy

*Cuninghame, Robt. Gun, Mount Kennedy, Newtownmountkennedy

*Dick, William Wentworth Fitzwilliam, M.P. *for co. Wicklow*, Humewood, Kiltegan; 20, Curzon-street, May Fair, London, W.; Carlton Club, London, S.W.; Sackville-street Club, Dublin

Fitzwilliam, Hon. Wm. Henry (was M.P. for co. Wicklow, 1868–74), Coolattin Park, Carnew; 4, Grosvenor-square, London, W.; Brooks's Club, London, S.W.

*Hodson, Sir George Frederick John, bart. (J.P. co. Dublin; High Sheriff co. Cavan, 1839; co. Westmeath, 1846), Hollybrook House, Bray; Greenpark. Mullingar; Athenæum Club, London, S.W.

Monck, Right Hon. Lord Viscount, G.C.M.G., P.C., *Lieutenant and Custos Rotulorum, co. of Dublin and co. of city of Dublin; a Commissioner of Church Temporalities and a Commissioner of National Education* (called to the bar, 1841; was M.P. for Portsmouth, 1852–57; a Lord of the Treasury, 1854–55; Governor-General of Canada, 1861–68), Charleville, Bray; Brooks's Club, London, S.W.

Powerscourt, The Right Hon. Lord Viscount, K.P. (elected a Representative Peer for Ireland, 1865; J.P. cos. Dublin, Tyrone, and Wexford; late Lieut. 1st Life Guards), Powerscourt Castle, Enniskerry; 65. Brook-st., London, W.; White's, Brooks's, and Marlborough Clubs, London, S.W.

*Synge, Francis, Glenmore Castle, Ashford

*Westby, Wm. Jones, M.A. (T.C.D.), (J.P. co. Carlow), High Park, Baltinglass; United Service Club, Dublin

Wicklow, Right Hon. Earl of (elected a Representative Peer for Ireland, 1872; late Lieut. 9th Lancers), Shel-

Magistrates.

*Ellis, Robert Francis, Seapark, Wicklow; Sackville-street Club, Dublin

Ellis, Thomas Cupples (J.P. co. Wexford), St. Austins, Inch, Gorey; Sackville-street Club, Dublin.

Esmonde, Lieut.-Col. Sir John, bart., *Waterford Militia Artillery*, M.P. *for co. Waterford* (J.P. and D.L. co. Wexford; J.P. co. Waterford; late Capt. Wexford Militia), D.L., Ballynastragh, Gorey, co. Wexford; Reform Club, London, S.W.

Fenton, Michael, Ballinclea, Donard; 15, Upper Sackville-street, Dublin

Finnemor, Samuel Ashworth, Ballyward, Kilbride

*Fitzsimon, Christopher O'Connell (J.P. co. Dublin), Glencullen, Golden Ball

Frizell, Charles, Castle Kevin, Annamoe

Greene, Francis William, Kilranalagh, Baltinglass

Owen, William, Blessington

Parnell, Charles Stewart, Avondale, Rathdrum

Patten, Robert, Clone, Aughrim; 25, Lower Fitzwilliam-street, Dublin

Pennefather, Edward, Q.C., B.A. (Oxon.), Rathsallagh, Dunlavin; 6, Fitzwilliam-place, Dublin; Kildare-street Club, Dublin

Posnett, George (J.P. cos. Down, Tyrone, and Wexford), Enniskerry, Bray

Powerscourt, Right Hon. Lord Viscount, K.P., D.L. (elected a Representative Peer for Ireland, 1865), (J.P. cos. Dublin, Tyrone, and Wexford; late Lieut. 1st Life Guards), Powerscourt Castle, Enniskerry; 65, Brook-street, London, W.; Brooks's, White's, and Marlborough Clubs, London, S.W.

Pratt, Fitzmaurice, Glenhest, Kilbride

These extracts from *Thom's County Directory*, 1875, indicate that Parnell held a position of some prominence among the gentry and aristocracy of Co. Wicklow.

Avondale

The townland of Avondale is on the west bank of the Avonmore River (Abhainn Mór) *from which it derives its name. The house dates from 1779 and was built for Samuel Hayes who then owned the estate. Hayes was greatly interested in forestry and was author of* A Practical Treatise on Planting Trees and Coppices *(1794). Many of the trees now in the demesne were planted by him.*

He was a keen amateur architect and may have designed the house himself. An unusual feature of the house was the two-storey entrance hall with a gallery along the inner wall. In Parnell's time, banners of the Irish Volunteers hung on the walls, and an old billiard-table stood in the centre.

The lofty entrance hall and gallery. (*Weekly Freeman*, 17 October 1891)

Avondale around Parnell's time.(E. Dickinson, *A Patriot's Mistake*)

The Parnell family coat-of-arms, with the motto, *Te digna sequere* – follow what is worthy of you. (NLI P&D)

CHAPTER II

Politics

According to his brother, John Howard, Parnell first became interested in political affairs during the American Civil War (1861-65). In this formative period of his life when the family was settled in Upper Temple Street in Dublin, his mother and his sister Fanny were outspoken supporters of the Fenian movement. At that stage he had little sympathy with the Fenians although, not surprisingly, he was outraged when the police searched the house for arms while he was away at Cambridge. But that same year, 1867, when the 'Manchester Martyrs' were hanged for their part in a rescue operation in which a police sergeant was killed, his attention became more firmly focussed on the Irish political situation.

However, it was not until some six years later when he had left Cambridge and was settled down to a relatively congenial life as squire of Avondale, that he seems to have considered becoming involved in politics. By then, he knew the limitations of his station in life, as the estate was heavily in debt and he was finding it difficult to make a living. With ancestors on both sides of the family who were prominent in public life, it was not surprising that, when considering career options, he should have taken some account of politics.

When the matter came to a head in 1874, he was already playing a role in the public life of the county as a magistrate and High Sheriff, offices which were almost exclusively the prerogative of the landed gentry and aristocracy. When entering politics, he would have been expected to seek a nomination from one or other of the two main British parties, the Liberals or the Conservatives. In the event, he sought election on a democratic ticket, as a representative of Isaac Butt's Home Rule League. This organisation included constitutional nationalists and a number of Liberals in its ranks. It campaigned for a limited measure of Home Rule whereby Ireland would have federal status within the British Empire.

While rallying to the nationalist cause, Parnell did not consider himself as in any sense a traitor to his class. Instead, he believed that the landed ascendancy was shortsighted in maintaining ultimately untenable positions on issues such as land reform and Home Rule. Moreover, he felt that, in their own long-term interests, the landlords should play the leading role in devising realistic solutions to the problems facing the country. He hoped that where he led, others of his class would follow, but in that belief he proved mistaken.

On a personal level, Parnell could not have expected to benefit materially from politics, at least in the short-term. Members of parliament were then unpaid, and attendance at Westminster involved such expense that, generally, only men of substantial private means stood for election. Indeed, when he was leader of the Irish Parliamentary Party, he had to contribute to the support of a number of his colleagues from his own limited resources.

The Dublin Election

At the general election of 1874 Parnell decided to stand for Co. Wicklow in the Home Rule interest. When he found that he was ineligible as he was High Sheriff for the county, he persuaded his brother, John Howard, to go forward instead. However, their campaign was not very effective and John Howard came in last of the three candidates.

Shortly afterwards, when there was a by-election for Co. Dublin, Parnell stood against the out-going Conservative candidate, Colonel T.E. Taylor. In his election address, Parnell drew attention to his ancestors. Contrary to his claim, Sir John Parnell was not a supporter of rights for Catholics, and his opposition to the Union was motivated by self-interest. But Parnell's grand-uncle, Sir Henry Brooke Parnell, did indeed promote the cause of Catholic Emancipation.

Co. Dublin was a bastion of Conservatism and Parnell was thought to have no chance. Nevertheless, he canvassed energetically and got a respectable poll of 1235 votes as against 2183 for Colonel Taylor.

A Fight for Dublin

On my return [from the United States] to England, I was present at the Rotunda when Charley delivered his first public speech as a candidate for Dublin. It had been carefully thought out and written down on paper at Mrs Dickinson's, in the top bedroom which he occupied there. The memorising of it occupied him during a whole sleepless night, and when he appeared at breakfast he seemed very tired. I may mention that it was Charley's invariable habit to think out his plans in detail while in bed at night.

When he delivered his speech, I was standing close by him. After a few sentences he stopped suddenly, apparently trying to recall a word which he had forgotten. He was not nervous, although the audience was. He seemed to search his brain deliberately for the missing word, disregarding all attempts on the part of friends to prompt him. When he had found it, we all realised that it was the only word to be fitly used in that connection. These pauses occurred several times during his speech, and no doubt gave rise to the impression among certain critics that he would never succeed as a public speaker. The whole-hearted applause of the audience, however, showed that, whatever the manner of his delivery, the matter of his speech had impressed itself on their minds.

His defeat did him no harm. As a matter of fact, by showing his dogged perseverance, it gained him

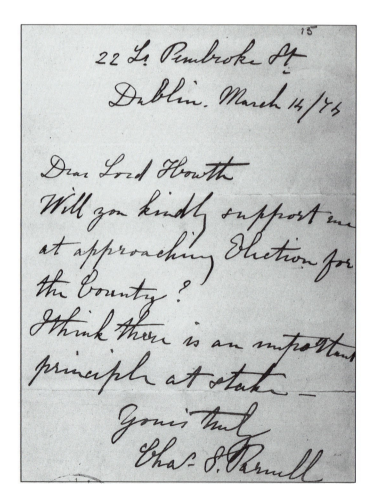

Letter to Lord Howth who was formerly a Liberal MP for Galway. (NLI MS 5934)

yet more ground with his party, and he became a man to be estimated by them and feared by their opponents.

(J.H. Parnell, *C.S. Parnell*, pp. 138-9)

To the Electors of the County of Dublin.

Gentlemen,

In compliance with influential requests, I offer myself as a candidate for your county at the approaching election.

Upon the great question of Home Rule, I will by all means seek the restoration to Ireland of our domestic Parliament, upon the basis of the resolutions passed at the National Conference of last November, and the principles of the Irish Home Rule League, of which I am a member. If elected to Parliament, I will give my cordial adherence to the resolutions adopted at the recent Conference of Irish Members, and will act independently alike of all English parties.

The wishes and feelings of the Irish nation are in favour of Religious Education. In these feelings I concur, and I will earnestly endeavour to obtain for Ireland a system of education in all its branches – University, Intermediate, and Primary – which will deal impartially with all Religious Denominations, by affording to every parent the opportunity of obtaining for his child an education combined with that religious teaching of which his conscience approves.

I believe security for his tenure and the fruits of his industry to be equally necessary to do justice to the tenant and to promote the prosperity of the whole community. I will, therefore, support such an extension of the ancient and historic Tenant Right of Ulster, in all its integrity, to the other parts of Ireland, as will secure to the tenant continuous occupation, at fair rents, and upon this subject, I adopt the declarations of the Tenant Right Conference held in Dublin on the 21st of last April and those made at Belfast on the 21st January.

I think the time has long since come when a complete and unconditional Amnesty ought to be extended to all the prisoners, without distinction, who are suffering for taking part in transactions arising out of political movements in Ireland. ...

If I appear before you as an untried man, my name and my family are not unknown in the history of Irish politics. My ancestor, Sir John Parnell, in the old Irish Parliament, was the active and energetic advocate of the removal of the disabilities which affected his Catholic fellow-countrymen. In the evil days of corruption which destroyed the independence of Ireland he lost a great office, and refused a peerage, to oppose the fatal measure of Union.

His successor, Sir Henry Parnell, rendered in the British Parliament services to the cause of Catholic Emancipation and of Ireland which the Irish people have not forgotten.

If you elect me, I will endeavour and think I can promise, that no act of mine will ever discredit the name which has been associated with these recollections.

I am, Gentlemen, Your faithful servant,

Charles Stewart Parnell, Avondale, 7th March, 1874.
(*Freeman's Journal,* 9 March 1874)

MP for Co. Meath

In April 1875 Parnell again stood for election to parliament, this time for Co. Meath. His election address was largely the same as that for Co. Dublin the previous year. He succeeded in getting the support of the Catholic clergy which proved decisive, and he was elected with a large majority.

The Irish Times *and other Conservative supporters took some comfort in the view that, while Parnell had deserted his own class and had defected to the Home Rule camp, at least his principles were thoroughly constitutional.*

Parnell took his seat in the House of Commons on 22 April 1875. In his maiden speech he opposed the coercive Peace Preservation (Ireland) Bill.

The Representation of Meath

On Monday a great county meeting was held in Navan for the purpose of nominating a fit and proper person to fill the seat made vacant in Parliament by the death of the late Mr John Martin. The occasion was one of particular interest, from the fact that it was expected the clergy would express their views on the subject in question, and that, in fact, the feeling of the county generally would be definitely indicated. A very large number of electors attended from the neighbouring districts, and the presence of bands of music, banners and bannerets gave the assemblage a most imposing look as they marched in order from the direction of the railway station through the town. Heading the procession, which formed shortly after the arrival of the morning train from Dublin, were Mr Charles Stewart Parnell, Mr T.D. Sullivan, Mr G.H. Kirk, MP; Mr P.N. Fay, MP, Mr James Cantwell, Mr Thomas Ryan & Co., and in front of them were carried two time-worn banners of the Irish Volunteers, the property of Mr Parnell, under which his ancestor had fought. ...

Mr Parnell, who, on coming forward, was received with immense cheering, expressed his thanks for the hearty welcome which he had received throughout the county, but especially in Navan. He said it might be thought that because he was a landlord he had no interest in the tenant, or might try to prevent the tenant having his interest in the land recognised by the State. If it were the wish of any landlord to come forward and say that his tenant has not as just and as good an interest in his farm as the landlord, such a possibility was rendered impracticable, and had been, in fact, removed by Mr Gladstone's Act of 1870. He was not going to praise Mr Gladstone's Act, for it had proved to be miserably inadequate (applause), and had, in some respects, done harm to the tenants, having converted some good landlords into bad ones, and because it had not given the slightest protection to the tenantry over three-quarters of Ireland. He, however, as a landlord, maintained that the tenant has property in the land as well as the landlord; and they should hold fast to that principle, and endeavour to pass a bill which would define what the interest of the tenant is, and which would protect that interest (applause). Without fixity of tenure and fair rents, the tenants would never be happy, nor would the country be prosperous. Therefore, he said, he was sure they would believe him that he would, in and out of Parliament, support 'fixity of tenure and fair rents'. With reference to the question of Home Rule, Mr Parnell said that since he first could think he had the principles of that movement very fixed in his heart, for he always believed that the day would come when the voice of the people in this country would rule her affairs and make her laws, and that was what he understood by Home Rule (applause).

(*Drogheda Argus,* 17 April 1875)

Mr Parnell ... He trusted that the time would arrive when the history of the past would be forgotten, so far as it reminded England that she was not entitled to Ireland's confidence, and when she would give to Irishmen the rights which they claimed – the right of self-government. Why should Ireland be treated as a geographical fragment of England, as he had heard an ex-Chancellor of the Exchequer call it some time ago. Ireland was not a geographical fragment, but a nation. He asked the House to regard Ireland as anxious to defend England when her hour of trial came; and he trusted the day might come when England might see that her strength lay in a truly independent, a truly free, and a truly self-supporting Irish nation.

(Hansard, *Parliamentary Debates*, 26 April 1875, 1645)

Parnell (no. 155) at the Bar of the House of Commons, waiting to take the oath, 22 April 1875. (Avondale)

Parliamentary Obstruction

By 1877 many of the Home Rule MPs had lost all faith in their ability to influence British policy on Ireland. In reaction, Parnell and a number of the more active members systematically obstructed the business of parliament, sometimes on matters of purely imperial concern. Their most notable action was in relation to the South Africa Bill in July-August 1877. On that occasion, by moving amendments and making very lengthy speeches, Parnell and six other Irish MPs succeeded in keeping the House in continuous session for twenty-six hours. The leader of the Home Rule group of MPs, Isaac Butt, repudiated this course of action, claiming that it was 'simply revolutionary' and that it alienated British good-will. However, it proved popular in Ireland and it helped to promote Parnell among the more radical elements of the Irish public.

Parliament: Commons

Mr Parnell, with characteristic imperturbability, was indulging in one of his long speeches, when first Mr Knatchbull Hugessen, and next Sir William Harcourt, the latter lashing himself into a white heat, called the hon. member for Meath to order. The equanimity of Mr Parnell was not to be disturbed by the rotund objurgations of the right hon. member for Oxford. He resolutely pursued his determined course of obstruction to the various clauses, acting in concert with Mr Biggar, Mr O'Donnell, Mr O'Connor Power, Mr Gray and Captain Nolan. To see the hon. member for Meath – a slender and rather good-looking young Irishman a little over thirty, with a determined cast of features and bearded as a pard – quietly rise time after time and, undeterred by the shouts and interruptions of angry Conservatives, unflinchingly

Isaac Butt (1813-79), leader of the Home Rule MPs. (*Illustrated London News*, 17 May 1879)

say his say, must have occasioned any stranger present the utmost surprise. Mr Parnell has the outward appearance of a gentleman. He is able, though obstinate. Nothing seems more surprising than that patriotism (with an emphasis on *pat*) should have thrown the hon. member for Meath into close companionship with Mr Biggar, whose uncouthness of speech and manner form a marked contrast to the refinement of Mr Parnell.

(*Illustrated London News*, 4 August 1877)

Joseph Gillis Biggar, MP for Co. Cavan, speaking in the House of Commons. Biggar pioneered the practice of 'retaliatory obstruction'. (*Illustrated London News*, 18 February 1882)

The Fenians

To ensure a broad political base, Parnell tried to attract the support of the more extreme nationalists. On occasion he made 'advanced' statements, but it is unlikely that he ever wished for complete separation from Britain or that he considered physical force as a viable option. However, as a matter of conviction, he advocated amnesty for the Fenian prisoners and he joined the Amnesty Association in 1876. That same year, he greatly impressed the Fenians when he opposed a government spokesman, Sir Michael Hicks-Beach, in the House of Commons on the issue of the Manchester Martyrs.

Isaac Butt had failed to achieve any worthwhile success in parliament and the extremists generally believed that Parnell would provide more dynamic leadership. By that stage the Home Rule Confederation of Great Britain, which Butt had founded in 1873, was largely dominated by members of the Fenian organisation, the Irish Republican Brotherhood, and in August 1877 Parnell was elected president.

Charley's Entrance into Politics

If the American Civil War may be said to have first aroused Charley's interest in politics, it was certainly the Fenian outbreak that concentrated that interest on Irish affairs. With the Fenian doctrine itself, and especially with the Fenian methods, he was never really in sympathy, though he used the great power of that well-organised body to effect his own ends, or, rather, to further that policy which he believed to be more beneficial to his country as a whole.

His loyalty to the Throne was above suspicion, though he always treated the English as open enemies and regarded their politicians with the utmost suspicion. Our mother, though American to the core, was a burning enthusiast in the cause of Irish liberty, and possessed of an inveterate hatred of England – against which country her famous father, Commodore Stewart, had so often waged battle with conspicuous success on the high seas – yet always instilled into her children the principles of personal loyalty to their Sovereign, which she held not to be inconsistent with individual liberty. ...

But if the cause of the Fenians did not enlist Charley's sympathies, the support which they received made him consider the abuses and distress which existed in his own country, which he saw more and more in their naked hideousness as he went about among his tenants on the Avondale estate.

It was the Manchester executions in 1867, however, that made the most marked impression on him. He vehemently declared that the killing of Sergeant Brett was no premeditated murder, but an accident – a declaration that he repeated with even more force to a startled House of Commons in 1875, when Sir Michael Hicks-Beach referred to those who perished on the scaffold as 'murderers'.

(J.H. Parnell, *C.S. Parnell*, pp. 127-9)

Sir Michael Hicks-Beach: There is another point on which I need hardly touch. It was mentioned by the hon. Member for Mayo [John O'Connor Power] – and, of all the extraordinary delusions which are connected with the subject, the most strange to me appears the idea that Home Rule can have the effect of liberating the Fenian prisoners, the Manchester murderers. ('No, no!') – I regret to hear that there is any hon. Member in this House who will apologize for murder.

Mr PARNELL: The right hon. Gentleman looked at me so directly when he said he regretted that any Member of this House should apologise for murder, that I wish to say as publicly and as directly as I can that I do not believe, and never shall believe, that any murder was committed at Manchester.

Sir MICHAEL HICKS-BEACH: If the hon. Gentleman believes that, I am sure I need not argue the question. I am stating not my own opinion, but the verdict of the jury who heard the evidence in the case. The Manchester murderers (Renewed cries of 'No, no!') committed a crime on English ground, of which they were convicted by an English jury, and for which they are detained in an English prison. How, then, I should like to know, can they be released by an Irish provincial Parliament?

(Hansard, *Parliamentary Debates*, 30 June 1876, 807-808)

THE HOME RULE CONFEDERATION

Banquet in Liverpool last night

(Special Telegram from our Correspondent)

Liverpool, Tuesday Night.

Today, the Home Rule Conference of Great Britain concluded the business after a five hours sitting. The position of president of the Home Rule Confederation for the year was, on the motion of Mr John Barry, Manchester, seconded by Mr Veldon, Liverpool, unanimously conferred on Mr C.S. Parnell, MP. The new president was warmly cheered on taking the chair. Messrs Biggar, MP, O'Donnell, MP, Commins, LLD, Barry and Ferguson were elected vice-presidents. It was resolved to hold the next annual convention in London during the sitting of Parliament. The Convention decided on issuing an address to the various towns and counties of Ireland, urging them to purify their national representation, and to require their members of Parliament to account to their constituents annually. ...

Mr Parnell, MP, rose to propose the next toast, 'The Home Rule Confederation and its Representatives.' He referred with gratitude to the encouragement he and Mr Biggar had derived from a demonstration like this in Liverpool last St Patrick's Day, when they had only just initiated a line of action of which they could not at the time display the results. ...

Alluding to the services of the Home Rule Confederation, he said they had no sordid interest in Ireland. ... What did they want? They wanted to break up the legislative functions of the present House of Commons and to redistribute them among small legislative assemblies responsible to the people who elected them. When Irish independence was brought about, other reforms would accompany it that would vitally benefit the people of Scotland and England. The so-called obstructives had not taken up a quarter of the time last session that ought to have been devoted to Irish legislation. Scotsmen and Englishmen would find next session that, little time as Parliament had this year to consider their affairs, they would have a great deal less time for the future (laughter), and they would find that they would have to join Irishmen in doing something better and stronger than grumbling if they wanted to get a remedy (cheers).

(*Freeman's Journal*, 29 August 1877)

The 'New Departure'

In 1870 Michael Davitt was sentenced to fifteen years penal servitude for Fenian activity. He was released on a ticket-of- leave in December 1877, mainly due to the efforts of Isaac Butt and Parnell. He resumed his Fenian connections and on 12 May 1878, on the train from London to St Helens, Lancashire, he invited Parnell to join the Irish Republican Brotherhood. Several years later, Davitt published an account of the incident.

Many Fenians in Ireland, Britain and the United States were impressed with Parnell's success in obstructing parliament. John Devoy, who was then leader of the Irish-American Fenian organisation, Clan na Gael, proposed that the Fenians abandon their traditional policy of repudiating all parliamentary activity. Instead, they should co-operate with Parnell and the other active MPs in achieving certain common goals. Devoy outlined the terms of this 'new departure' in a telegram to the Freeman's Journal *but Parnell made no public response.*

Charles Stewart Parnell

I saw him a few times again before my departure for America in July 1878. We were travelling from London to a town in Lancashire where an amnesty meeting was to be held. It was in the month of May. I asked him to join the revolutionary organisation; not, however, to subscribe to the silly oath of secrecy or to become a mere figure-head in a do-nothing conspiracy. ...

Not a word had my auditor spoken during the talk of which this is a summary from notes made at the time, but on my concluding, he quietly but instantly said: 'And what next?' There was a note of friendly scepticism in the question which my answer did not modify. He then said, slowly but clearly: 'No, I will never join any political secret society, oath-bound or otherwise. It would hinder and not assist me in my work for Ireland. Others can act as seems best for themselves. My belief is that useful things for our cause can be done in the British Parliament in proportion as we can get reliable men to join us and follow a resolute policy of party independence. We must endeavour to re-establish faith in parliamentary work of an earnest and honest kind, and try in this way to secure the good-will of men like yourself who are justified in doubting from past experience whether any real service can be rendered to the Irish people by electing representatives to go to Westminster. I agree with a good deal of what you suggest about putting a stronger programme before the public, especially in relation to the land question, and I see no reason why men who take opposing views as to the best way of liberating Ireland cannot work in harmony for minor reforms.

(M. Davitt, *Fall of Feudalism*, pp. 111-113)

Michael Davitt (1846-1906), born at Straide, Co. Mayo. (M.Davitt, *Leaves from a Prison Diary*)

John Devoy (1842-1928), born at Kill, Co. Kildare. (*Devoy's Postbag*, vol.ii)

The Fenian Brotherhood and Mr Parnell, MP

The following is a copy of a despatch cabled to Dublin from New York, and signed by men who will be accepted as representatives of the advanced Irish National party in the United States. It is addressed to Mr Parnell and his political friends, but before reaching them it will be submitted to a number of representative Nationalists in Dublin for their approval:–

'The Nationalists here will support you on the following conditions:–

First – Abandonment of the Federal demand, and substitution of a general declaration in favour of self-government.

Second – Vigorous agitation of the land question on the basis of a peasant proprietary, while accepting concessions tending to abolish arbitrary eviction.

Third – Exclusion of all sectarian issues from the platform.

Fourth – Irish members to vote together on all imperial and home questions, adopt an aggressive policy, and energetically resist coercive legislation.

Fifth – Advocacy of all struggling nationalities in the British Empire and elsewhere.'

An answer to the above despatch is expected in a day or two, when the Nationalists in America will decide what form their action will take.

(*Freeman's Journal*, 11 November 1878)

Supplement Gratis with "THE UNION." Saturday, 29th January, 1887.

PARNELL.—"PLAY HOME RULE."
AMERICAN CONSPIRATOR.—"SEPARATION'S OUR GAME."

Throughout his career, Parnell's unionist opponents believed he was criminally involved with extremists. This cartoon shows him dictating to Gladstone who is playing chess with the Prime Minister, Lord Salisbury.

Entry into Politics

While on occasion Parnell angled for the support of extremists, he frequently reiterated his commitment to constitutional politics. In his evidence to the Special Commission in 1889, he recalled his reasons for first entering politics. He was under examination by his junior counsel, H.H. Asquith (Prime Minister 1908-1916). His evidence should be regarded with caution as he was then trying to distance himself from extremism and wished to create the impression that he always had a mature and responsible attitude.

The Special Commission

Mr Charles Stewart Parnell, MP, sworn; examined by Mr Asquith.

58,247. I believe until the year 1874 you took no active part in public affairs? – Scarcely at all. I took a little part in the general election preceding the passage of the Irish Church and Land Acts, in favour of the Liberal candidate for the county of Wicklow.

58,248. Were you already interested in social and political questions in Ireland? – I cannot say I was very much interested in political questions at that time. I had been observing matters, but I was chiefly attending to my own private business.

58,249. Do you remember the Fenian rising in 1867? – Yes. I recollect that of 1865 and subsequent years. I was at Cambridge then. I watched the course of that movement with some interest and attention. ...

85,251. Do you remember the passing of the Ballot Act in 1872? – Yes. The passing of the Ballot Act in 1872 was the first public event which more intimately directed by attention to politics. I thought that arising out of the passage of that Act, that the political situation in Ireland was capable of very great change. I had some knowledge, not a very deep knowledge, of Irish history, and had read about the Independent Opposition movement of Sir Charles Gavan Duffy and the late Mr Frederick Lucas in 1852, and whenever I thought about politics, I always thought that that would be an ideal movement for the benefit of Ireland.

58,252... How did the passing of the Ballot Act affect the situation? – The passing of the Ballot Act, in my opinion, rendered it possible for Ireland to have, to some extent, an independent party reflecting the opinions of the masses of the people.

58,253. Why was that – what was the change? – Acting independently in the House of Commons, free from the influence of either English political party; pledged not to take office, or form any combination with any English political party until the wants of Ireland had been attended to. The passing of the Ballot Act rendered this possible, in my judgement, because for the first time it enabled the Irish electors to vote free from the coercion of their landlords. Up to that time the electors had, to a great extent, been driven in like sheep to the polls, and in many cases where they resisted the wishes of their landlords, they were fined heavily by the imposition of extra rent and in other cases dispossessed from their holdings for the exercise of the franchise.

58,254. About this time – that is about the time of the passing of the Ballot Act, did Mr Butt and others form the Home Rule League? – Mr Butt, just subsequently to the passage of the Ballot Act and prior to the General Election of 1874, formed the Home Rule League and succeeded in returning 59 members, pledged, according to the principles of the Independent Opposition party in 1852, to remain aloof from all English political parties, to form an independent separate party in the House of Commons, to refuse office until the just rights of Ireland in the direction of a native legislature were conceded. ...

(Special Commission, 1888, Minutes of Evidence (1890), xii, 1-2)

CHAPTER III

The Land War

When Parnell entered politics in the mid-1870s, one of the most serious national problems was the issue of landlord-tenant relations. Over the centuries the agrarian system had been developed by the landlords, and the law generally protected their interests. The whole system retarded the development of the economy, it caused widespread hardship, and for generations it was a chronic source of recrimination, crime and civil disorder.

As a landlord and an MP representing a rural nationalist constituency, Parnell was well placed to understand the complexities of landlord-tenant relations. He was aware of the garrison mentality of the landlords and of their conviction that they could only maintain their position by taking strong action against any resistance by the tenants. He was also conscious that, in the economic circumstances of the time, many landlords were finding it difficult to make a living from their estates and that, to survive, they would have to take radical action. On the other hand, the Parnells had a good relationship with their tenants for generations, and he was personally on familiar terms with many of them. He appreciated their difficult situation and, within limits, he was well disposed towards helping to improve their lot.

By the time Parnell came on the political scene, the Fenians had focussed the attention of the government on Irish grievances in a dramatic fashion, and as a result the balance of power had begun to shift away from the landlords. First, they had the psychological shock of the disestablishment of the Church of Ireland. Then, in 1870, Gladstone's Liberal government passed the first land act ever to improve the situation of the tenant at the expense of the landlord. Their position was further eroded with the Ballot Act of 1872. This introduced secret voting at elections and enabled the tenants to elect MPs on whom they could rely to represent their interests. Moreover, by that date most of the tenants had been educated in the national schools, they were conscious of their rights and were articulate in asserting them.

As a landlord, Parnell had to appear positive in his attitude to the tenant farmers. He acknowledged his commitment in his address to the electors of Co. Dublin in 1874, a commitment which he reiterated in most of his speeches in the following years. His general stance was along the lines of the 'three Fs' – fair rent, fixity of tenure and free sale. He believed that reform should be mainly to the tenants' advantage but, at that stage, he did not favour the notion that landlordism should be abolished and the tenants transformed into proprietors.

The land question became critical in the late 1870s due to an economic depression in Britain and a succession of bad harvests at home. In April 1879 a new wave of agrarian agitation was initiated at Irishtown in Co. Mayo by the former Fenian prisoner, Michael Davitt. Parnell was interested but for some time he remained cautious about getting involved. He knew that an agrarian movement would be difficult to control and that it could be taken over by extremists. However, he was also aware that it was an opportunity to broaden his base and to enhance his status within the active wing of the parliamentary party and in the country as a whole.

The Land League

On 8 June 1879, on the invitation of Michael Davitt, Parnell addressed a tenants' meeting at Westport, Co. Mayo. It had been denounced by Dr McHale, Archbishop of Tuam, on the grounds that it was likely to promote agrarian outrage. At that stage the agitation was being organised mainly by Fenian activists and Parnell took a considerable risk in becoming involved. However, his attendance at Westport gave the campaign some impetus, and two months later the National Land League of Mayo was established. Davitt then prevailed upon Parnell to become president of a national agrarian movement. He accepted the responsibility on the understanding that the programme would be strictly constitutional.

The Irish National Land League was established on 21 October 1879. Its aims were to bring about a reduction of rack-rents and, in the long term, 'to facilitate the ownership of the soil by the occupiers'. The committee included activists from the old Tenants' Defence organisations, eight MPs, some priests, and a number of Fenians and former Fenians. Among these were Davitt, Biggar, Thomas Brennan and Patrick Egan who became the mainstay of the whole operation.

The Great Tenant-Right Meeting at Westport

Mr Parnell, MP, who was loudly cheered, in proposing the second resolution said he wished to refer to the letter of his Grace, the Archbishop of Tuam, which had appeared in the *Freeman's Journal*. He need not tell them that it would ill-become him, or anybody else, to treat anything proceeding from a man who had stood, as his Grace had, between the Irish people and the exterminator, with anything but the highest respect. This meeting had been placarded throughout the County Mayo for some six or seven weeks, announcing that he (the speaker) and other public men would address it. During all those weeks not a single person in Mayo or out of it, no clergyman ever intimated to him that the Archbishop was opposed to this meeting.

3

Committee:

CHARLES STEWART PARNELL, M.P., President, Avondale, Rathdrum.

Purcell O'Gorman, M.P., Waterford.	O. J. Carraher, Cardestown, Co. Louth.
John Ferguson, Glasgow.	J. White, P.P., Milltown-Malbay.
W. Quirke, P.P., Dean of Cashel.	P. Cummins, P.L.G., Rathmines.
A. Cummins, LL.D., Liverpool.	James Daly, P.L.G., Castlebar.
Mathew Harris, Ballinasloe.	P. M. Furlong, C.C., New Ross.
Ulick J. Canon Bourke, P.P., Claremorris.	Thomas Ryan, Gt. Brunswick-street, Dublin.
J. O'Connor Power, M.P., London.	James Rourke, Gt. Britain-street, Dublin.
John Behan, C.C., Francis-street, Dublin.	Richard Kelly, "Tuam Herald."
Richard Lalor, Mountrath.	William Dillon, Nth. Gt. George's-street, Dublin.
J. L. Finegan, M.P., London.	I. J. Kennedy, T.C., Clonliffe-terrace, Dublin.
R. Sheehy, C.C., Kilmallock.	M. O'Flaherty, Dunoman Castle, Croom.
J. J. Louden, B.L., Westport.	John Sweetman, Kells.
O'Gorman Mahon, M.P., London.	M. F. Madden, Clonmel.
John Dillon, North Great George's-street, Dublin.	J. C. Howe, London.
W. Joyce, P.P., Louisburgh, Co. Mayo.	Thomas Lynch, P.P., Painstown, Beauparc.
N. Ennis, M.P., Claremount, Co. Meath.	J. F. Grehan, P.L.G., Cabinteely, Co. Dublin.
Thomas Roe, "Dundalk Democrat."	D. Brennan, P.P., Kilmacow, Co. Kilkenny.
J. R. M'Closkey, M.D., Derry.	W. Kelly, Donabate, Co. Dublin.
George Delany, Burlington-road, Dublin.	C. Reilly, Artane, Co. Dublin.
T. D. Sullivan, "Nation," Dublin.	L. M'Court, P.L.G., Bolton-street, Dublin.
James Byrne, Wallstown Castle, Cork.	Stephen O'Mara, Limerick.
J. E. Kenny, 71, Lr. Gardiner-street, Dublin.	Thomas Grehan, Loughlinstown, Co. Dublin.
Mulhallen Marum, J.P., Ballyragget.	M. K. Dunne, C.C., Enniscorthy.
P. F. Johnston, Kanturk.	M. J. Kenny, P.P., Scariff.
M. Tormey, C.C., Painstown, Beauparc.	R. H. Medge, Athlumney House, Navan.
Thomas Canon Doyle, P.P., Ramsgrange.	Michael A. Conway, P.P., Skreen, Co. Sligo.
Philip J. Moran, Finea, Granard.	

Treasurers:

W. H. O'Sullivan, M.P., Kilmallock. | J. G. Biggar, M.P., Belfast. | Patrick Egan, 25, Synnot-place, Dublin.

Honorary Secretaries:

A. J. Kettle, P.L.G., Artane, Co. Dublin.	Thomas Brennan, 6, Russell-street, Dublin.
Michael Davitt, 83, Amiens-street, Dublin.	

Committee Rooms,
62, Middle Abbey Street, Dublin.

Extract from a brochure issued by the Land League in 1880. (NLI ILB 343, Briefs 2)

A Voice – 'It was never him who wrote the letter'.

Mr Parnell – It was only when leaving my home yesterday to come here that I, for the first time, became acquainted, by reading that letter, that his Grace was opposed to the meeting. I am sure 'John of Tuam' would not wish me to dishonour myself by breaking my word to this meeting and by remaining away from it (applause). ...

I am one of those who believe the landlord institution is not a natural institution in any country. I believe that the maintenance of the class of landlords in a country is not for the greatest benefit of the greatest number. Ireland has, perhaps, suffered more than any other country in the world from the maintenance of such a class. England has, perhaps, assimilated itself better than any other country to the landlord system; but in almost every other country in the world where the system has been tried, it has been given up. In Belgium, in Prussia, in France and in Russia, the land has been given to the people – to the occupiers of the land. In some cases, the landlords have been deprived of their property in the soil by the iron hand of revolution; in other cases, as in Prussia, the landlords have been purchased out. If such an arrangement could be made without injuring the landlord, so as to enable the tenant to have his land as his own, and to cultivate it as it ought to be cultivated, it would be for the benefit and prosperity of the country. I look to this as the final settlement of this question, but in the meanwhile, it is necessary to ensure that, as long as the tenant pays a fair rent, he shall be left to enjoy the fruits of his industry. A fair rent is a rent the tenant can reasonably pay according to the times but in bad times, a tenant cannot be expected to pay as much as he did in good times three or four years ago (applause). If such rents are insisted upon, a repetition of the scenes of 1847 and 1848 will be witnessed. Now, what must we do in order to induce the landlords to see the position? You must show the landlords that you intend to hold a firm grip of your homesteads and lands (applause). You must not allow yourselves to be dispossessed, as you were dispossessed in 1847. ...

(*Connaught Telegraph*, 14 June 1879)

The executive committee of the Land League in session; from left: Patrick Egan, Hon. Treasurer; T.D. Sullivan, MP; John Dillon, MP; C.S. Parnell, MP, President; two reporters; Thomas Sexton, MP; Michael O'Sullivan, Assistant Secretary; Thomas Brennan, Secretary; J.G. Biggar, MP; T.M. Healy. (*The Graphic*, 27 November 1880)

Tour of United States

In December 1879 the Land League dispatched Parnell and John Dillon to America to collect funds for the relief of distress in the west of Ireland. Dillon had Fenian contacts and John Devoy and Clan na Gael supported the tour. Parnell addressed meetings at over sixty venues and collected over £70,000. He tended to temper his speeches to his audience and, on occasion, he seemed to advocate complete separation from England. As a result he found favour with the more extreme Irish-Americans.

The relatively rare privilege of addressing the United States Congress was granted to Parnell, mainly due to the influence of Clan na Gael. In his speech he confined himself to the agrarian issue and proposed that the landlords be bought out, if necessary by compulsion.

Office IRISH FAMINE RELIEF FUND,

Room 59, No. 32 Park Place,

New York, January 30th, 1880.

Sir:

We beg to enclose you copy of an Appeal which we have issued to the American People. The circumstances of the case are of so pressing and so terrible a nature, that we trust they will form a sufficient excuse for addressing you.

We would venture to suggest the immediate formation of a Relief Committee in your city, composed of gentlemen of all Nationalities, so that an opportunity may be afforded every citizen of assisting us to keep our people alive until the Government of England comes to their relief.

All money sent to Drexel, Morgan & Co., will be cabled promptly to Ireland, and used within a week, in saving the Peasantry of the West of Ireland from death by starvation.

Yours, truly,

CHARLES S. PARNELL,
JOHN DILLON.

A leaflet from the Devoy Papers. (NLI MS 18,041)

IN CONGRESS – WASHINGTON
Mr Parnell's Speech

He said – Mr Chairman and Gentlemen of the House of Representatives, I have to thank you for the distinguished honour you have conferred upon me in permitting me to address this august assembly upon the state of affairs in my unhappy country. The public opinion of the people of America will be of the utmost importance in enabling us to obtain a just and suitable settlement of the Irish question. I have seen since I have been in this country so many tokens of the good wishes of the American people towards Ireland, I feel at a loss to express my sense of the enormous advantage and service which is daily being done to the cause of my country. ... Many of us who are observing now the course of events believe that the time is fast approaching when the artificial and cruel system prevailing in Ireland is bound to fall and be replaced by a more natural and more just one (applause). I could quote many authorities to show you what this system is. The feudal tenure has been tried in many countries, and it has been found wanting everywhere, but in no country has it wrought so much destruction and proved so pernicious as in Ireland. ...

Now, Mr Speaker and Gentlemen of the House of Representatives, the remedy that we propose for the state of affairs in Ireland is an alteration of the land tenure prevailing there. We propose to imitate the example of Prussia and of other continental countries where the feudal tenure has been tried, found wanting, and abandoned; and we propose to make or give an opportunity to every tenant occupying a farm in Ireland to become the owner of his own farm (applause). ...

(*Irish World*, 14 February 1880)

Detail from an address presented to Parnell by the Land League on his return from the United States; illustrated by Thomas J. Lynch. (NLI P&D)

PARNELL ADDRESSING THE UNITED STATES HOUSE OF REPRESENTATIVES IN SESSION. WASHINGTON, FEBY 2ND 1880.

Chairman of Party

In the general election of April 1880 Parnell was returned for three constituencies, including Cork City which he opted to represent. He also managed to get a number of his supporters elected and so increased his following within the parliamentary party. The following month he succeeded in winning the chairmanship from the holder, William Shaw, who had succeeded Isaac Butt the previous year. As chairman, Parnell exercised strict discipline over the party and transformed it into an effective force in parliament.

The Irish Parliamentary Party

The adjourned meeting of Irish Home Rule members of parliament was held at the City Hall yesterday. At the commencement of the meeting, forty-five members were present, and apologies were received from ten gentlemen. The proceedings commenced at 12 o'clock. ...

The Lord Mayor – We have now the original resolution, proposed by Mr Brooks and seconded by Mr Richard Power, that Mr Shaw be elected sessional chairman; and the amendment, moved by The O'Gorman Mahon and seconded by Mr Biggar, that Mr Parnell be elected as sessional chairman. I will put first the amendment, that Mr Parnell be elected. His Lordship then put the amendment and upon a division the following voted. For the amendment – Messrs Sexton, T.P. O'Connor, O'Kelly, Byrne, Barry, McCarthy, Biggar, A.O'Connor, Lalor, T.D. Sullivan, Leamy, O'Sullivan, Commins, Gill, Dawson, Leahy, Corbet, McCoan, Finigan, Daly, Marum, O'Gorman Mahon, O'Shea – 28. Against – McFarlane, Brooks, Colthurst, Synan, O'Brien (Sir Patrick), Foley, Smithwick, Fay, Errington, Gabbett, Smyth, Richard Power, Blake, McKenna (Sir Joseph), Martin, Meldon, Callan and the Lord Mayor – 18.

The Lord Mayor declared the amendment carried, and then put it as an original resolution, viz. – That Mr Parnell be elected sessional chairman. He declared the 'ayes' had it. ...

Mr C.S. Parnell (who was received with applause) – My Lord Mayor, I was prevented by the sudden apparition of lunch from expressing my obligations to the Irish party for the very distinguished honour which they have conferred upon me. The functions of chairman were strictly defined and limited by resolutions adopted some

Parnell in 1880. (*Illustrated London News*, 20 November 1880)

years since unanimously by the party. They do not imply in any sense leadership of the party, and I do not wish it to be supposed by the country that the Irish party, in conferring the high and honourable position of chairman upon me, have in any way entrusted me with the leadership of the party ('hear, hear'). It is true that they have conferred upon me the highest and most honourable office at their disposal ('hear, hear'). I cannot but feel proportionately gratified and

Charles James Patrick, The O'Gorman Mahon (1800-91). A noted duellist and adventurer, he was an O'Connellite MP for Co. Clare, which he again represented when he proposed Parnell for chairman in May 1880. (*T.M. Healy, Letters*, vol.i)

Joseph Gillis Biggar (1828-90); a Belfastman and MP for Co. Cavan, he seconded the nomination of Parnell for chairman. (*Illustrated London News,* 20 November 1880)

honoured by this trust. Of course, the responsibility of such a trust is a very great one, and I could have wished that some other arrangement could have been made, and that some gentleman – neither Mr Shaw nor myself – should have been selected for the office, and that in that way a unanimous vote of the party should have been obtained. I may say I made early this morning a proposition directed to that effect in favour of Mr Justin McCarthy. I think it right to make this known in order to show that I have not sought this office in any way, and should have very much preferred that somebody else had accepted it. I am sensible that it must tie my hands to a very considerable extent in the future, and that possibly my utility may be diminished in that way. But, as I have been honoured in this way, I cannot undertake the responsibility of refusing the trust which has been offered to me, and I may say that I hope to prove myself to a certain extent worthy of the very high trust which has been offered to me. I certainly consider myself unworthy of that trust, but I hope to merit the good opinion to a certain extent of my friends by my conduct as your chairman ('hear, hear'). ...

(*Freeman's Journal,* 18 May 1880)

Ennis and Limerick

Throughout 1880 branches of the Land League were established around the country. Most sections of the nationalist community supported the movement, including many of the Catholic clergy and the Fenian rank-and-file. Parnell was constantly on the move addressing meetings and rallies in cities and towns. He was also extremely active in parliament and achieved a notable success in June 1880 when the new Gladstone administration introduced a bill providing compensation for evicted tenants. However, it was rejected by the House of Lords in August. Probably in reaction to this set-back, on 19 September at Ennis, Co. Clare, Parnell advocated the use of non-violent intimidation which became one of the Land League's most effective tactics. Due to its success against Captain Charles Boycott at Lough Mask, Co Mayo, the term 'to boycott' became common language.

The Ennis Demonstration

Mr Parnell: ...It depends, therefore, upon yourselves and not upon any commission or any government. When you have made this question ripe for settlement, then, and not till then, will it be settled (cheers). It is very nearly ripe already in many parts of Ireland. It is ripe in Mayo, Galway, Roscommon, Sligo and portions of the County Cork (cheers). But I regret to say that the tenant farmers of the County Clare have been backward in organisation up to the present time. You must take and band yourselves together in Land Leagues. Every town and village must have its own branch. You must know the circumstances of the holdings and of the tenures of the district over which the League has jurisdiction – you must see that the principles of the Land League are inculcated, and when you have done this in Clare, then Clare will take her rank with the other active counties, and you will be included in the next land bill brought forward by the government (cheers). Now, what are you to do to a tenant who bids for a farm from which another tenant has been evicted?

Several voices: 'Shoot him'.

Parnell addressing a rally at Limerick, 1 November 1880. (*The Graphic,* 13 November 1880)

In acknowledgement of Parnell's leading role in the agrarian movement, he was conferred with the Freedom of the City of Limerick on 2 November 1880. (*The Graphic*, 13 November 1880)

Mr Parnell: I think I heard somebody say, 'shoot him' (cheers). I wish to point out to you a very much better way – a more christian and charitable way, which will give the lost man an opportunity of repenting (laughter, and 'hear, hear'). When a man takes a farm from which another has been evicted, you must shun him on the roadside when you meet him – you must shun him in the streets of the town – you must shun him in the shop – you must shun him in the fair-green and in the market place, and even in the place of worship, by leaving him alone, by putting him into a moral Coventry, by isolating him from the rest of his country as if he were the leper of old – you must show him your detestation of the crime he has committed. If you do this, you may depend on it there will be no man so full of avarice – so lost to shame – as to dare the public opinion of all the right-thinking men in the county and transgress your unwritten code of laws. People are very much engaged at present in discussing the way in which the land question is to be settled, just the same as when a few years ago, Irishmen were at each other's throats as to the sort of parliament we would have if we got one. I am always thinking it is better first to catch your hare before you decide how you are going to cook him (laughter). I would strongly recommend public men not to waste their breath too much in discussing how the land question is to be settled, but rather to help and encourage the people in making it, as I said just now, ripe for settlement (applause). When it is ripe for settlement you will probably have your choice as to how it shall be settled, and I said a year ago that the land question would never be settled until the Irish landlords were just as anxious to have it settled as the Irish tenants (cheers).

A voice: 'They soon will be'.

Mr Parnell. There are, indeed, so many ways in which it may be settled that it is almost superfluous to discuss them; but I stand here to-day to express my opinion that no settlement can be satisfactory or permanent which does not ensure the uprooting of that system of landlordism which has brought the country three times in a century to famine. The feudal system of land tenure has been tried in almost every European country and it has been found wanting everywhere; but nowhere has it brought more exile, produced more suffering, crime and destitution than in Ireland (cheers). ...

(*Freeman's Journal*, 20 September 1880)

The 'Traversers'

As the agrarian agitation intensified, outrages and general lawlessness increased. The government feared that the situation was drifting towards revolution, and decided to take legal action against the leaders of the Land League. On 2 November 1880, Parnell and thirteen others were charged with seditious conspiracy and they were brought to trial in January 1881. However, as Dublin Castle no longer had the power to pack juries, the jury disagreed and the case collapsed. The defendants were generally referred to as the 'traversers' – in effect this legal term meant that they were pleading 'not guilty'.

The Irish State Trials

The indictment charges these persons with a conspiracy; first, to impoverish and injure the owners of farms let to tenants for rent; secondly, conspiracy to impede and frustrate the administration of justice and the execution of legal writs for levying of moneys due for rent or for recovery of land on non-payment of rent; thirdly, conspiracy to prevent the taking of any farm from which a tenant has been evicted; fourthly and lastly, conspiracy to excite discontent and dis-affection among the Queen's subjects, with ill-will and hostility between different classes – that is to say, between landlords and tenants in Ireland. The unlawful means of this conspiracy are particularly described. They are stated to be, the soliciting and procuring large numbers of tenants to refuse payment of rents due; deterring them from paying rent by threatening them with public hatred and contempt; with exclusion from social intercourse and business; with annoyance and injury and with violence to their persons and property; also, procuring an agreement to frustrate the sale of goods lawfully seized for rent; and instigating tenants who were evicted to resist the execution of the law, and to retake possession of the farms. Menaces and acts of violence are said to have been used, to the great terror and alarm of the landlords, and 'against the peace of our Sovereign Lady the Queen, her Crown and dignity.' There are nineteen counts in the indictment.

(*Illustrated London News,* 8 January 1881)

This print from an original by W.T. Parkes shows the defendants seated in the second row down from the judges with Parnell in the centre. (Dublin Civic Museum)

SUPPLEMENT TO THE WEEKLY FREEMAN OF 18TH DEC., 1880.

PORTRAITS OF THE FOURTEEN TRAVERSERS
IN THE
STATE PROSECUTION
OF THE
LAND LEAGUE.

MATTHEW HARRIS.
from Photo. by Chancellor.

PATK EGAN.
from Photo. by Wm Laurence.

JOHN DILLON.
from life.

T. D. SULLIVAN.
from Photo. by Wm Laurence.

J. W. NALLY.
from American Photo.

JOSEPH GILLIS BIGGAR.
from Photo. by Wm Laurence.

CHAS STEWART PARNELL.
from a Photo. by Henry O'Shea, Limerick.

P. J. SHERIDAN.
from Photo. by Nelson Bros, Sligo.

JOHN. W. WALSHE.
from Photo. by A. & G. Taylor.

THOS SEXTON.
from Photo. by Wm Laurence.

P. J. GORDON.
from Photo. by T. J. Wynne, Castlebar.

T. BRENNAN.
from Photo. by Chancellor.

M. P. BOYTON.
from Photo. by Wm Laurence.

MICHL M. O'SULLIVAN.
from Photo. by Wm Laurence.

35

Parnell and His Tenants

Parnell's opponents frequently alleged that, while he campaigned for the rights of tenant farmers, he was himself an unscrupulous landlord who rack-rented his tenants. However, this is contradicted by the record as illustrated by two contemporary newspaper items.

Reduction of Rents

Henry Shepard Esq., Oatlands, County Wicklow has, unasked, made the liberal abatement to his tenants of 20 per cent on the current year's rent ending 25th of March, 1880.

Mrs Andrew William Byrne, Croneybyrne, Rathdrum, has given 10 per cent reduction to her tenants on her estate at Knockanany, Ballinasillogue, Knockanooher, Ardnaboy and Knocknashea, Co. Wicklow.

Mr Charles Stewart Parnell, MP, has granted a reduction of 20 per cent off this year's rent, and has given bog leave to all his tenants.

(*Wicklow Newsletter*, supplement, 15 November 1879)

MR PARNELL AND HIS TENANTS

Remarkable Testimony

The following has appeared in the *Freeman:*

Sir – We, the undersigned tenants residing on Mr Parnell's property in the townlands of Blackrock, Carrignamuck, Carrignameel and Aughavanagh, in the County of Wicklow, and parish of Hacketstown, hereby protest in the strongest possible terms against the false statements and cowardly slanders constantly uttered from the bench in Hacketstown court, and from the chair in Baltinglass boardroom, by a JP (Colonel Dennis).

We hereby declare that Mr Parnell is treating us, his tenants, exactly according to his public declarations made at public meetings attended by him.

Mr. PARNELL

AS

A LANDLORD

AND A

"LAND-GRABBER."

The title of a pamphlet published by the main landlord organisation, the Irish Loyal and Patriotic Union, c. 1885.

We are only asked to pay Griffith's valuation and are not asked for arrears. If the reductions in rent given us of late years have not reduced our rent to Griffith's valuation, we will be allowed the difference at next payment of rent.

We humbly implore the assistance of the *Freeman's Journal* to have public opinion brought to bear on the scandalous conduct of the above-named magistrate, in order to secure his removal from the bench of the Hacketstown court of justice, where those insults offered to Mr Parnell in his absence (as cowards will), and in the presence of Mr Parnell's tenants, who take them as offered to themselves, are well calculated to destroy our confidence in the administration of justice. Signed,

Martin Byrne, Aughavanagh; Michael Kehoe, Carrignameel; Edward Dwyer, do; James Byrne, do; Matthew Kavanagh, do; Michael Dwyer, do; James (his x mark) Shiel, do; Edward Farrel, do; James (his x mark) Byrne, Blackrock; Patrick Byrne, do; James Neill, do; Michael Whealon, do; John Toole, Aughavanagh; James Fallon do; Laurence Fallon, do; Ann Whealon, Carrignameel; George Whitty, Carrignamuck; James Coogan, do; John Dempsey, do; John Coogan, do; Thomas Deegan, do; Michael Fallon, Aughavanagh.

(*The Nation*, 27 November 1880)

CHAPTER IV

Katharine O'Shea

When he was twenty-five years of age Parnell fell in love with an American girl whom he met in Paris. He pursued her to her home in the United States but she eventually rejected him. Thereafter, he seems to have had no serious involvement with women until he met Katharine O'Shea in July 1880 when he was thirty-four. At that time Katharine had been living apart from her husband, Captain William O'Shea, for about five years.

In April 1880 O'Shea was elected to parliament as a Home Rule MP for Co. Clare. He regarded Parnell as too 'advanced', but he voted for him in the election for chairmanship of the party. Presumably, he hoped to derive some personal benefit from an association with him, and it was partly on his initiative that the relationship between Parnell and his wife developed. O'Shea must have been aware of the nature of the relationship from an early stage, but he seems to have become reconciled to the situation. He had political dealings with a number of prominent members of the Liberal party, especially Joseph Chamberlain, and he hoped that the liaison between his wife and Parnell would give him a role as an intermediary between Parnell and the Liberals.

There was also another factor which was probably more important. O'Shea had only limited private means and depended on his wife for his living expenses. Katharine, herself, was completely supported by a wealthy aunt, Mrs Benjamin Wood (Aunt Ben), who was expected to leave her a large legacy. As Aunt Ben was then in her late eighties, O'Shea probably believed that his best course was to defer a final break at least until Katharine had inherited and was in a position to make him a worthwhile settlement.

At the same time, Katharine could not divorce her husband as it would jeopardise the legacy. Parnell had to accept the situation as tacitly understood by the other two. Moreover, he could not afford to outrage his Roman Catholic followers by getting involved in a divorce scandal. As it turned out, within a couple of years many of his Irish parliamentary colleagues knew of the affair, as did members of the Cabinet, including Gladstone and Chamberlain.

Parnell did not have strong religious beliefs and he was not at all concerned about the moral aspects of the relationship. He considered that Katharine's marriage to O'Shea was no longer valid and that he was justified in becoming involved with her. Indeed, he seems to have felt that, apart from the legal technicality of not having their union registered, they were in fact married. Their life together seems to have been harmonious and extremely domesticated. They had three children, all girls, but the first who was born in February 1882 while Parnell was in Kilmainham Jail died in infancy. Katharine helped out as his unofficial secretary, and on a number of occasions acted as an intermediary with Gladstone and the Liberals. Regarding their private life, practically the only source of information is her book, _Charles Stewart Parnell: His Love Story and Political Life,_ which was published in 1914.

The O'Sheas

Katharine O'Shea was a daughter of Sir John Page Wood who was rector of a parish in Essex. The family were well connected and an uncle, Lord Hatherley, was Lord Chancellor in Gladstone's first government. In 1867, at the age of twenty-one, she married William O'Shea, who was formerly a captain in the 18th Hussars. O'Shea was a Catholic and the son of a wealthy Dublin solicitor. He had some property in Ireland and mining interests in Spain, but was generally impecunious and depended on his wife for support. The marriage failed and the couple lived apart from about 1875. Katharine and their three children resided at Eltham, about seven miles from London, while William had an apartment at Victoria. He usually called out to Eltham on Sundays and took the children to Mass.

Though they no longer lived together, Katharine (or rather her Aunt Ben) continued to support O'Shea, and she paid the expenses arising from his election for Co. Clare. To further his career, she occasionally held dinner parties at St Thomas' Hotel in Berkeley Square to which she invited his political associates.

Captain William O'Shea (1840-1905). (*Illustrated London News,* 10 July 1880)

Katharine O'Shea (1845-1921). 'This portrait was coloured for Mr Parnell in 1880 and always carried by him until his death'. (K. O'Shea, *C.S. Parnell,* vol.i)

The First Meeting with Mr Parnell

We gave several dinners, and to each of them I asked Mr Parnell. Among the first to come were Mr Justin McCarthy (the elder), Colonel Colthurst, Richard Power, Colonel Nolan and several others; but, in spite of his acceptance of the invitation, Mr Parnell did not come. Someone alluded to the 'vacant chair' and laughingly defied me to fill it; the rest of our guests took up the tale and vied with each other in tales of the inaccessibility of Parnell, of how he ignored even the invitations of the most important political hostesses in London and of his dislike of all social intercourse, though he had mixed freely in society in America and Paris before he became a politician for the sake of the Irish poor. I then became determined that I would get Parnell to come, and said, amid laughter and applause: 'The Uncrowned King of Ireland shall sit in that chair at the next dinner I give!'.

One bright sunny day when the House was sitting, I drove, accompanied by my sister, Mrs Steele (who had a house in Buckingham Gate), to the House of Commons and sent in a card asking Mr Parnell to come out and speak to us in Palace Yard.

He came out, a tall, gaunt figure, thin and deadly pale. He looked straight at me smiling, and his curiously burning eyes looked into mine with a wondering intentness that threw into my brain the sudden thought: 'This man is wonderful – and different.'

I asked him why he had not answered my last invitation to dinner, and if nothing would induce him to come. He answered that he had not opened his letters for days, but if I would let him, he would come to dinner directly he returned from Paris, where he had to go for his sister's wedding.

In leaning forward in the cab to say good-bye, a rose I was wearing in my bodice fell out on to my skirt. He picked it up and, touching it lightly with his lips, placed it in his button-hole.

This rose I found long years afterwards, done up in an envelope with my name and the date, among his most private papers, and when he died, I laid it upon his heart.

(K. O'Shea, *C.S. Parnell,* i, 135-6)

Wonersh Lodge, Eltham, Mrs O'Shea's house, where Parnell lived for many years. It was provided for her by her Aunt Ben who had a mansion nearby. (K. O'Shea, *C.S. Parnell*, vol. i)

Parnell in 1880; a photograph by his nephew, Henry Thomson, which he gave to Mrs O'Shea soon after their first meeting. (K. O'Shea, *C.S. Parnell*, vol. i)

The Affair Begins

Parnell first met Katharine O'Shea in July 1880. Some months later, on Captain O'Shea's invitation, he moved into Wonersh Lodge for a short period. On his visits to Ireland he wrote to Katharine, and by October the tone of the letters had become intimate. Thereafter, he spent much of his time at Wonersh Lodge. He did his best to keep the affair secret, but within a year Captain O'Shea was probably aware of the nature of the relationship.

Dublin, Tuesday [September].

My Dear Mrs O'Shea, – I have just a moment on my return from Ennis to catch the late post and reply to your wire.

I received your two letters quite safely and you may write me even nicer ones with perfect confidence. I blame myself very much for not having written you on my way through Dublin on Saturday, as you were evidently anxious about your notes, but I hope you will forgive me as there were only a few minutes to spare.

I trust to see you in London on Tuesday next. Is it true that Captain O'Shea is in Paris, and, if so, when do you expect his return? ... [*sic*] I have had no shooting, weather too wet, but shall try tomorrow, when you may expect some heather.

Dublin, Monday evening, October 17, 1880.

My own love, – You cannot imagine how much you have occupied my thoughts all day and how very greatly the prospect of seeing you again very soon comforts me.

On Monday evening I think it will be necessary for me to go to Avondale; afterwards I trust, if things are propitious on your side, to return to London on Tuesday or Wednesday.

Yours always, C.

– Two letters (the first unsigned) from Parnell to Mrs. O'Shea.

(K. O'Shea, *C.S. Parnell*, i, 149)

Photographs of Katharine O'Shea from the period 1865-1914. (*Daily Sketch,* 20 May 1914)

At Eltham

In the autumn of 1880 Mr Parnell came to stay with us at Eltham, only going to Dublin as occasion required. Willie had invited him to come, and I got in some flowers in pots and palms to make my drawing-room look pretty for him.

Mr Parnell, who was in very bad health at that time, a few days later complained of sore throat, and looked, as I thought, mournfully at my indoor garden which I industriously watered every day. It then dawned upon me that he was accusing this of giving him sore throat and I taxed him with it. He evidently feared to vex me, but admitted that he did think it was so, and 'wouldn't it do if they were not watered so often?' He was childishly touched when I at once had them all removed, and he sank happily on to the sofa, saying that 'plants were such damp things!'

His throat became no better, and he looked so terribly ill when, as he often did now, he fell asleep from sheer weakness on the sofa before the fire, that I became very uneasy about him. Once, on awaking from one of these sleeps of exhaustion, he told me abruptly that he believed it was the green in the carpet that gave him sore throat. There and then we cut a bit out and sent it to London to be analysed, but without result. It was quite a harmless carpet.

During this time I nursed him assiduously, making him nourishment at regular intervals, seeing that these day-sleeps of his were not disturbed, and forcing him to take fresh air in long drives through the country around us. At length I had the satisfaction of seeing his strength gradually return sufficiently to enable him to take the exercise that finished the process of this building-up, and he became stronger than he had been for some years. I do not think anyone but we who saw him then at Eltham, without the mask of reserve he always presented to the outside world, had any idea of how near death's door his exertions on behalf of the famine-stricken peasants of Ireland had brought him. ...

In the early summer of 1881, my aunt had one of her old friends to stay with her, and I seized the opportunity of freedom to take my children to Brighton for a month, after settling the old ladies

Parnell after his beard was shaved off. (K. O'Shea, *C.S. Parnell*, vol. i)

together. I had gone down before the children to take rooms for them, and was walking across Brighton Station when I was suddenly joined by a tall man whom I did not recognise for a moment until he said quietly, 'don't you know me?' It was Mr Parnell, who had slipped into the train at Clapham Junction, knowing that I was going to Brighton, and who had cut off his beard with his pocket scissors in the train in order to avoid being recognised at Brighton. He had wrapped a white muffler round his throat, and pulled it as high as possible over the lower part of his face, with the result that the manageress of the hotel he stayed at was certain that he had an infectious illness of the throat, and rather demurred at letting him in. It was only by the expedient of complaining loudly at being kept waiting in the draught with his 'raging toothache' that 'Mr Stewart' was reluctantly admitted. I could not bear his appearance – neither bearded nor shaven – so he went off soon after arrival, was properly shaved, and relieved the hotel staff by discarding the muffler and assuring them that he was free from pain now his 'tooth' was out.

He went to Cork soon after this and, to please me, was photographed without the beard and with the ring I had given him on his finger.

Note: Here, as elsewhere, Katharine O'Shea's dating is probably incorrect; a number of portraits show Parnell without his beard before the end of 1880.

(K. O'Shea, *C.S. Parnell*, i, 149-53, 181-2)

The Eltham Resident

As his relationship with Katharine O'Shea developed, Parnell spent much of his time at Wonersh Lodge and visited Avondale less often. He even had his horses taken across and stabled nearby in Eltham. To ensure that his new abode was congenial, Katharine had a cricket pitch laid out in the garden. She also had a study and a laboratory added to the house where he could indulge his hobby of assaying rocks from Avondale. To some extent, Katharine assisted him with his paper-work and on occasion acted as his intermediary with Gladstone and the Liberals. Some of his colleagues who knew of the relationship believed that she exerted considerable influence on him regarding political matters.

Astronomy

During his leisure moments at Eltham, Mr Parnell took up the study of astronomy with the vigour that always characterised him when he was interested in a subject. He had picked out from my bookshelf a book of stars – one of Sir Robert Ball's, I believe, that I had bought at random one day, and became at once interested. From the teaching of an old friend of my father's I had a fairly good knowledge of astronomy, and, though by no means well up in the latest research and discoveries, I was able to tell him much of the stellar systems that was new to him. Finding how he devoured the little book of Sir Robert Ball's, I got several of the latter's interesting works for him, besides Herschel's.

Then Mr Parnell told me of a magnificent telescope he had at Avondale and sent for it. When this arrived, he sent for a few sacks of Portland cement, with which he made a pedestal in my garden, and himself mounted the telescope upon it. He made an ingenious arrangement whereby the slightest touch would tilt the telescope to the desired angle, and we spent many nights, he and I, watching the stars and following the courses of the planets till they faded in the dawn. Then he thought of how near to us was the Observatory at Greenwich, and got a permit to go over the Observatory. After that, on the days when my aunt had her readers with her, I used to accompany him to the Observatory, where we spent many hours. He could always absorb very quickly any knowledge that appealed to him, and he soon had the pleasure of teaching me much about the latest discoveries, and about a subject intensely interesting to him – the wonderful way in which the telescopes used in the great observatories of the world are made.

In time this study of the stars began to worry him too much, and he reluctantly gave up all serious work on the subject. He said it was all too immense and absorbing to think about in a life that was primarily concerned with politics. But the pedestal remained, and still we occasionally

A photograph of Parnell taken in the sitting-room at Wonersh Lodge by Katharine O'Shea in 1886. (K. O'Shea, *C.S. Parnell*, vol. i)

mounted the telescope and kept vigil with the stars through the summer night.

Horses and Dogs

In 1885 I had a new room built on to my house at Eltham, adjoining my sitting-room and leading into the greenhouse and thence to the garden. Parnell and I took the greatest interest in the building of this room; he superintended every detail, saw that the cement was laid to the proper depth under the flooring, and sent to Avondale for sufficient sweet-chestnut wood to have the room panelled half-way up and to make beautiful, heavy double-doors, window settings, and the mantlepiece and fittings. It was a very comfortable and warm room when finished, and to celebrate its completion – it was to be Parnell's own study and workroom – I photographed him in it, sitting in his own special easy chair, surrounded by his assaying paraphernalia and holding his pestle and mortar. ...

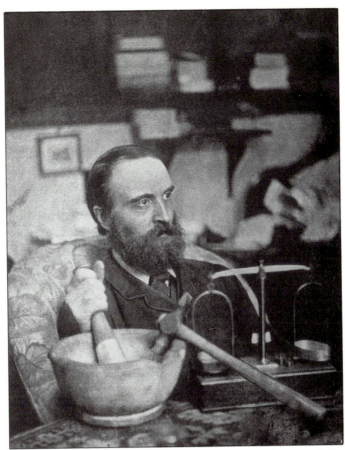

Parnell in his laboratory at Wonersh Lodge. (E. Dickinson, *A Patriot's Mistake*)

Parnell on horseback at Eltham. (K. O'Shea, *C.S. Parnell*, vol ii)

Parnell rented some stables fairly near my house for his horses and took much interest in their welfare. He was not a man who had very much knowledge of horses, but he was a fine horseman, and on his hunter, President, a beautiful horse of sixteen hands and a weight-carrier, he looked remarkably well. He took a scientific interest in the shoeing of the horses and, to the great annoyance of his grooms, would constantly try new methods of shoeing in order to deaden the 'jar' of the contact of the road.

This trial of new methods proved a boon to my horse, Dictator, given me by Parnell, for the tenderness of his feet was completely cured when Parnell, dead against the conservative ideas of my stableman, insisted on his having leathers inserted between Dictator's foot and shoe.

(K. O'Shea, *C.S. Parnell*, i, 192-3, ii, 74)

Katharine's Recollection

Parnell as I Knew Him

When I first met Mr Parnell in 1880 he was unusually tall and very thin. His features were delicate with that pallid, pearly tint of skin that was always peculiarly his. The shadows under his deep, sombre eyes made them appear larger than they were, and the eyes themselves were the most striking feature of his cold, handsome face. They were a deep brown, with no apparent unusualness about them except an odd compulsion and insistence in their direct gaze that, while giving the impression that he was looking through and beyond them, bent men unconsciously to his will. But when moved by strong feeling, a thousand little fires seemed to burn and flicker in the sombre depths, and his cold, inscrutable expression gave way to a storm of feeling that held one spellbound by its utter unexpectedness.

His hair was very dark brown, with a bronze glint on it in sunlight, and grew very thickly on the back of his shapely head, thinning about the high forehead. His beard, moustache and eyebrows were lighter brown. His features were very delicate, especially about the fine-cut nostrils; and the upper lip short, though the mouth was not particularly well shaped. His was a very handsome, aristocratic face, very cold, proud and reserved; almost all the photographs of him render the face too heavy and thicken the features.

He had an old-world courtliness of manner when speaking to women, a very quiet, very grave charm of consideration that appealed to them at once in its silent tribute to the delicacy of womanhood. I always thought his manner to women, whether equals or dependents, was perfect. In general society he was gracious without being familiar, courteous but reserved, interested yet aloof, and of such an unconscious dignity that no one, man or woman, every took a liberty with him.

In the society of men his characteristic reserve and 'aloofness' were much more strongly marked, and even in the true friendship he had with at least two men, he could more easily have died than have lifted the veil of reserve that hid his inmost feeling. I do not now allude to his feeling for myself, but to any strong motive of his heart – his love for Ireland and of her peasantry, his admiration that was almost worship of the great forces of nature – the seas and the winds, the wonders of the planet worlds and the marvels of science.

(K.O'Shea, *C.S. Parnell*, ii, 238-9)

Parnell's daughters: Clare (1883-1909),who strongly resembled him, and Katharine - Katie - (1884-1947). Another daughter, Sophie Claude, was born and died in 1882. The children were, of course, generally known as O'Sheas. (Kilmainham Jail)

CHAPTER V

Kilmainham Jail

In the spring of 1881 as the Land War was about to enter a new phase, Parnell might well have been satisfied with the progress of the previous eighteen months. In October 1879, when the agitation was in its infancy, he had displayed considerable courage in becoming involved in what was by no means a popular cause. His bold initiative in speaking at Westport and then assuming the presidency had given the Land League some political credibility and raised its profile at national level. Under his direction it had become a mass-movement with the support of virtually all shades of nationalist opinion. On the political front the organisation was now effectively represented in parliament. In 1879 Parnell had only the support of a small group of activists, but at this stage he was leader of the majority of the Home Rule MPs at Westminster. Moreover, unlike any nationalist leader since Daniel O'Connell, he had succeeded in imposing discipline and control on his followers, and he now led a united group of MPs with a clear identity and a common purpose.

Within the Land League itself Parnell had managed to retain control. Although the organisation hovered on the brink of illegality and on occasion outrages were perpetrated by the rank and file, he was able to restrain the drift towards extremism, and the Land League remained in essence a constitutional organisation. There was chronic tension between moderates and extremists, but Parnell kept the movement together and maintained his position as the dominant figure.

In 1881 Gladstone's Liberal administration resorted to a traditional British strategy of coercion followed by appeasement. Following the collapse of its case against the 'traversers' in January, it secured formidable powers of internment without trial in March. However, while coercion on its own was not likely to pacify the country, Gladstone hoped that his Land Act would satisfy enough tenants to make the Land League largely redundant. The Act conceded the 'three Fs' and provided a land court to adjudicate on rents. Parnell and the moderates were satisfied with the Act but for tactical reasons he publicly opposed it. He compromised by recommending that the land court be tested by submitting a number of carefully selected cases.

Faced with Parnell's apparent rejection of the Land Act, Gladstone resorted to internment, and Parnell and several of the other leaders were imprisoned without trial. Parnell then went along with the extremists and called for a general rent strike. However, he probably realised that at that stage it was a futile gesture as most of the tenants were likely to ignore the strike and apply to the land court to get their rents favourably adjusted. Also, he must have foreseen that the call for a rent strike would result in the suppression of the Land League, a prospect which he may indeed have welcomed. In his view the tenants had gained most of what they were entitled to, the Land League had served its purpose, and it was time for a return to a more orthodox line of politics.

Suspension from the Commons

In December 1880 Parnell succeeded in imposing greater control over the majority of the Home Rule MPs. Thereafter, they sat as a group on the opposition benches and generally acted in consort. As a result, in January 1881 he was able to slow down the progress of the coercive Protection of Persons and Property (Ireland) Bill through the House of Commons. In reaction, the procedures of the House were amended and the possibilities for delaying tactics became more limited. This particular phase of obstruction reached a climax on 3 February when it was announced that Michael Davitt's ticket-of-leave had been suspended. John Dillon and Parnell launched a protest, and thirty-six Irish MPs were suspended in succession.

However, Parnell evaded pressure from his more extreme supporters to escalate the campaign by taking the revolutionary step of withdrawing from Westminster and leading his group of MPs home to Ireland to organise a total rent strike.

The Silent Member

...At any rate, Mr Parnell, in his iciest tone, demanded of the Home Secretary which of the conditions of his ticket-of-leave Mr Davitt had broken. ...But Mr Gladstone simply rose to make his motion. The right hon. gentleman, however, was not allowed to complete his first sentence. One of the most obstinate of the Land League members, Mr Dillon, persisted in claiming a hearing, resolutely stood with folded arms, and absolutely refused to budge when bidden to resume his seat. The Speaker had no alternative but to 'name' Mr Dillon, in accordance with the standing orders of last spring; Mr Gladstone quietly moved that the hon. member be suspended for the sitting; and Mr Dillon was thereupon suspended by 395 to 33 votes. Mr Dillon, however, would not leave until removed by 'superior force'; and kept his seat until the Serjeant-at-Arms, Captain Gosset, had summoned a few of the doorkeepers to his aid.

The Prime Minister again rose after Mr A.M. Sullivan had relieved himself of some of the inflated rhetoric he has in stock; but again Mr Gladstone was interrupted, this time by Mr Parnell, with a demand that the right hon. gentleman be no longer heard. Mr Parnell was in his turn 'named' and suspended; but he and his companions kept their seats, and declined to take part in the division. The numbers were 405 to 7, a majority of 398 in favour of Mr Parnell's expulsion. But he, like Mr Dillon, refused to stir unless removed by 'superior force' – which being forthcoming in the persons of Captain Gosset and his subordinates, Mr Parnell readily accompanied the Serjeant-at-Arms, bowed respectfully to the Speaker, and left the House, amid the indignant exclamations of his supporters. Posing or posturing is a passion with these impulsive Irish members. It is needless, therefore, to state how they gloried in posing as martyrs and strained the patience of the House until the last of them was removed by 'superior force'. The remainder whom Lord R. Grosvenor had to name to the Speaker as having refused to vote, and the Home-Rulers previously withdrawn, are included in this list of Irish members suspended on Thursday se'nnight:–

Mr Dillon, Mr Parnell, Mr Barry, Mr Biggar, Mr Byrne, Mr W. Corbet, Mr Gray, Mr Healy, Mr Dawson, Mr Finigan, Mr Gill, Mr Lalor, Mr Leamy, Mr Leahy, Mr McCarthy, Mr McCoan, Mr Marum, Mr Metge, Mr Nelson, Mr A. O'Connor, Mr T.P. O'Connor, The O'Donoghue, The O'Gorman Mahon, Mr O'Sullivan, Mr O'Connor Power, Mr Redmond, Mr Sexton, Mr Smithwick, Mr A.M. Sullivan, Mr T.D. Sullivan, Mr Molloy, Mr R. Power, Mr O'Shaughnessy, Mr O'Donnell and Mr O'Kelly.

(*Illustrated London News,* 12 February 1881)

Parnell's suspension from the House of Commons, 3 February 1881. (*Daily Graphic*, 6 December 1890)

Gladstone's Land Bill

The Land League realised much of its original programme with Gladstone's Land Bill of 7 April 1881 which conceded 'the three Fs', that is a fixed period of tenure, free sale of the tenant's interest in the property (the 'Ulster Custom') and fair rents. It provided a land court to arbitrate on rents and it established the Land Commission to operate a hire-purchase scheme in cases where landlords wished to sell out to the tenants. In general, the Bill was satisfactory, and it established the important principle of dual ownership of the land in that both landlord and tenant now had a saleable interest in the property.

While Parnell and most moderates regarded the Bill as a reasonable settlement, he opposed it for tactical reasons. By taking a hostile stance he hoped to have it amended, and after it became law in August he focussed his criticism on the land court to ensure that it acted impartially. However, his main concern was to retain his influence with the more extreme wing of the Land League which feared that the measures would satisfy the tenants and so end the agitation. At the National Land Convention on 15-17 September, Parnell succeeded in getting both moderates and extremists to agree to test the Act by submitting trial cases to the land court. The moderates believed that the tests would prove the Act satisfactory, while the extremists hoped that it would be exposed as inadequate.

SUPPLEMENT TO THE "WEEKLY FREEMAN"   APRIL 16TH 1881.

THE GENIUS OF THE BILL.

The above Picture accurately represents the "powerful influences" under which Mr. Gladstone drafted his new Land Bill.

The Parnell of Kilmainham

But the National Convention was about to assemble, and everybody except Parnell was in a state of some perturbation as to the result. ... In a huge assembly, apparently in a fever of revolutionary enthusiasm, where not a single speaker was heard to advocate anything but the rejection of the Act, neck and crop, and where Parnell, when he rose to speak at the end of the debate, was received with a frozen silence and seemed to have scarcely a partisan left in the National Convention, none even of his parliamentary lieutenants presenting himself to say a word in favour of testing the unpopular Act, the great leader, in a speech of the prosiest good sense, brought the whole turbulent assembly all but unanimously to his own conclusion. The 'Kilmainham Party', who at one moment seemed to dominate the Convention, when the tellers were named for a division accepted in silent submission the overwhelming show of hands that declared for Parnell's policy.

The next three weeks witnessed a series of scenes which exhibited Parnell at the meridian height of his power as a leader of men. After a few days' rest in his Wicklow home, testing the gold washings of the river that ran through his demesne; or pondering over his pet problems in trigonometry, he made a triumphant entry into Dublin, with a hundred thousand men all but tearing him and one another limb from limb in the paroxysms of their frantic allegiance. It was after midnight when he escaped from their wild embraces. By the morning train he was on his way to a county convention in Maryborough; the next day he addressed the Central Branch of the Land League; a night afterwards he was at the head of the multitude who welcomed Father Sheehy on his release from Kilmainham Jail; within the same week he was in the midst of the most exciting scene of all, among his own constituents of Cork City, of all the hot Keltic race, the hottest in their ecstasies and the most bewitching in their clinging tenderness. In the midst of all this round of intoxicating excitements, he applied himself steadily to the work of sifting out his test cases for the land courts. Before or after one of those speeches, every sentence of which was scanned by hundreds of thousands of hostile eyes, he would break away from the excited admirers who beset his hotel, and shut himself up with some shrewd attorney or cool-headed local captain, working out the intricate particulars of scores of suggested claims, with a view to lighting upon those that would be most likely to eventuate in a satisfactory standard of rent for the different classes of tenancy.

(William O'Brien, *Parnell*, pp. 17-19)

Parnell addressing the National Land Convention at the Rotunda, Dublin. He was well aware of the power of the press, and in August 1881 he established the weekly newspaper, *United Ireland,* with William O'Brien , MP as editor.

Prison

In the autumn of 1881 the government believed that the situation was getting out of control. The Land Act had failed to reduce tension, the level of outrage was on the increase, and Parnell was bitterly critical of Gladstone. The Chief Secretary, W.E. Forster, advocated firm action, and it was decided to intern the Land League leaders under the provisions of the Protection of Persons and Property Act. Parnell was arrested at Morrison's Hotel in Dawson Street, Dublin, on 13 October 1881. The warrant charged him with 'inciting other persons wrongfully and without legal authority to intimidate diverse persons with a view to compel them to abstain from doing what they had a legal right to do, namely to apply to the Court under the provisions of the Land Law (Ireland) Act, 1881, to have a fair rent fixed for their holdings'.

Parnell's living conditions in Kilmainham were reasonably comfortable but the enforced confinement did not suit him and his health deteriorated. He was attended by Dr J.E. Kenny, MP, a fellow internee.

Morrison's Hotel, Dublin.

October 13, 1881.

My own Queenie, – I have just been arrested by two fine-looking detectives and write these words to Wifie to tell her that she must be a brave little woman and not fret after her husband.

The only thing that makes me worried and unhappy is that it may hurt you and our child.

You know, darling, that on this account it will be wicked of you to grieve, as I can never have any other wife but you, and if anything happens to you I must die childless. Be good and brave, dear little Wifie, then. Your Own Husband.

Politically, it is a fortunate thing for me that I have been arrested, as the movement is breaking fast, and all will be quiet in a few months, when I shall be released.

– The detectives who arrested Parnell allowed him to write a letter to Katharine and post it on the way to Kilmainham. At the time she was pregnant with their first child which was born the following February.

(K. O'Shea, *C.S. Parnell*, i, 206)

Parnell's arrest and arrival at Kilmainham Jail. (*The Graphic*, 22 October 1881)

Extract from Doctor Kenny's
Journal —
                15th November 1881.

I am becoming more Seriously
alarmed Concerning the Condition
of Mr. Parnell's health, He has
lost his appetite almost Completely
Sleeps very badly and Suffers
much from the Sciatica, — He is
rapidly loosing flesh and
appearance, the Confinement evident
=tly telling on him very heavily.
If I do not find a Change for
the better within the next day or
So I shall Consider it my duty
to ask for further professional
assistance.

Fanny and Anna Parnell

The Land League responded to the arrest of its leaders by calling for a 'no rent' campaign. The government then suppressed the Land League but the agitation was continued to some extent by the Ladies' Land League. This organisation was first established in the United States in 1880 by Parnell's sister Fanny for the purpose of raising funds, and his sister Anna directed it in Ireland.

The Ladies' Land League

Miss Anna Parnell was a lady of remarkable ability and energy of character – fragile in form, of medium height, dark-brown hair and kindly eyes, the handsome Parnell face, with all her great brother's intense application to any one thing at a time, and with much more than even his resoluteness of purpose in any enterprise that might enlist her interest and advocacy, together with a thorough revolutionary spirit. ...

The plans which the Ladies' League were to put in operation were these: Offices would be provided for their executive at the headquarters of the Land League proper, which had been removed in December from Middle Abbey Street to 39 Upper O'Connell Street, Dublin. Miss Parnell and her lieutenants would be supplied with duplicate addresses of League branches everywhere, at home and abroad, and would be put in communication with the local leaders of the organisation in every county and district in Ireland. The duty of supporting evicted tenants would fall to their work, and of encouraging resistance to land-grabbing. Wooden huts were to be provided, and if possible as near the evicted holding as ground for their erection would be found available; this for shelter, but also to enable the evicted family to keep a vigilant watch over their interests in the vacant farm. Another very important task was the support of families while members of the same would be in prison.

(M. Davitt, *Fall of Feudalism,* p. 300)

The Ladies' Land League office with Anna Parnell (1852-1911) at her desk. She was more extreme than her brother. After his release from Kilmainham, he suppressed the organisation and their relationship became strained. (*The Graphic*, 12 November 1881)

Hold the Harvest

Now are you men, or are you kine, ye tillers of the soil?
Would you be free, or evermore, the rich man's cattle, toil?
The shadow on the dial hangs that points the fatal hour –
Now hold your own! or, branded slaves, forever cringe and cower.

The serpent's curse upon you lies – ye writhe within the dust;
Ye fill your mouths with beggar's swill, ye grovel for a crust;
Your lords have set their blood-stained heels upon your shameful heads,
Yet they are kind – they leave you still their ditches for your beds!

Oh, by the God who made us all – the seignior and the serf –
Rise up! and swear this day to hold your own green Irish turf!
Rise up! and plant your feet as men where now you crawl as slaves,
And make your harvest fields your camps, or make of them your graves!

– Stanzas from Fanny Parnell's famous poem which Michael Davitt regarded as 'the Marseillaise' of the Land League.

(R.M. Mc Wade, *C.S. Parnell*, p.57)

Fanny Parnell (1849-82), Parnell's favourite sister; she was an accomplished poet. In her latter years she lived with her mother at 'Ironsides', Bordentown, New Jersey, the Stewarts' family home. (*The Nation*, 5 March 1881)

While Parnell was imprisoned in Kilmainham his supporters ploughed and manured his estate farm at Avondale.
(*Illustrated London News*, 7 January 1882)

The 'Kilmainham Treaty'

Parnell was probably to some extent relieved when he was imprisoned and the Land League suppressed. He believed that the organisation had served its purpose and that in time the tenants would accept the Land Act as a satisfactory settlement. In the meantime his major concern was the condition of Katharine O'Shea. She was then pregnant with their first child, Sophie Claude, who died some weeks after birth.

By the spring of 1882 the government realised that the internment of Parnell had in fact resulted in an escalation of crime and civil disorder. It decided to reach an accommodation with him, and Captain O'Shea was used as an intermediary. The terms of the eventual understanding, the so-called 'Kilmainham Treaty', were outlined in a letter from Parnell to O'Shea. The government undertook to improve the 1881 Land Act by extending it to leaseholders and by providing remission of rent arrears. Parnell on his part was to use his influence to end the agitation.

Letter from Parnell to Katharine O'Shea. (K. O'Shea, *C.S. Parnell*, i, 226-7)

Kilmainham,
April 28.

I was very sorry that you had left Albert Mansions before I reached London from Eltham, as I had wished to tell you that after our conversation I had made up my mind that it would be proper for me to put McCarthy in possession of the views which I had previously communicated to you. I desire to impress upon you the absolute necessity of a settlement of the arrears question which will leave no recurring sore connected with it behind, and which will enable us to show the smaller tenantry that they have been treated with justice and some generosity.

The proposal you have described to me as suggested in some quarters, of making a loan, over however many years the payment might be spread, should be absolutely rejected for reasons which I have already fully explained to you. If the arrears question be settled upon the lines indicated by us, I have every confidence – a confidence shared by my colleagues – that the exertions which we should be able to make strenuously and unremittingly would be effective in stopping outrages and intimidation of all kinds.

As regards permanent legislation of an ameliorative character, I may say that the views which you always shared with me as to the admission of leaseholders to the fair rent clauses of the Act are more confirmed than ever. So long as the flower of the Irish peasantry are kept outside the Act there cannot be any permanent settlement of the land question, which we all so much desire.

I should also strongly hope that some compromise might be arrived at this season with regard to the amendment of the tenure clauses. It is unnecessary for me to dwell upon the enormous advantages to be derived from the full extension of the purchase clauses, which now seem practically to have been adopted by all parties.

My dear Mr O'Shea
I think this very good

Yours very truly
Chas S Parnell
Kilmainham Dec 19 -1881

Parnell in 1881; by Henry O'Shea, a Limerick photographer. (Mrs Ann Fitzgerald)

The accomplishment of the programme I have sketched would, in my judgement, be regarded by the country as a practical settlement of the land question, and would, I feel sure, enable us to co-operate cordially for the future with the Liberal Party in forwarding Liberal principles; so that the Government, at the end of the session, would, from the state of the country, feel themselves thoroughly justified in dispensing with further coercive measures. – Yours very truly,

C.S. Parnell.

– Letter from Parnell to Captain O'Shea setting out the terms of the 'Kilmainham Treaty'.

(K. O'Shea, *C.S. Parnell,* i, 238-9)

The Phoenix Park Murders

Parnell was released on 2 May and the Chief Secretary, W.E. Forster, resigned in protest. Four days later the new Chief Secretary, Lord Frederick Cavendish and the Under Secretary, Thomas Burke, were assassinated in Dublin by a militant group known as 'The Invincibles'. Parnell, Dillon and Davitt immediately issued a statement condemning the outrage, a step which antagonised the more extreme nationalists.

As a result of the assassinations, the cooperation between Parnell and the Liberals suggested by the 'Kilmainham Treaty' did not materialise. The government introduced a new coercion bill which Parnell strenuously opposed in parliament. However, it did honour its commitment regarding arrears, and the Arrears Act, which became law in August, virtually ended the Land War of 1879-82.

The Manifesto of the Chiefs to the People of Ireland

On the eve of what seemed a bright future for our country, that evil destiny which has apparently pursued us for centuries has struck another blow at our hopes which cannot be exaggerated in its disastrous consequences. In this hour of sorrowful gloom we venture to give an expression of our profound sympathy with the people of Ireland in the calamity which has befallen our cause through a horrible deed, and with those who had determined at the last hour that a policy of conciliation should supplant that of terrorism and national distrust. ... We appeal to you to show, by every manner of expression possible, that amidst the universal feeling of horror which the assassination has excited, no people are so intense in their detestation of its atrocity, or entertain so deep a sympathy for those whose hearts must be seared by it, as the nation upon whose prospects and reviving hopes it may entail more ruinous effects than have yet fallen on the lot of unhappy Ireland during the present generation.

We feel that no act had ever been perpetrated in our country during the struggle for social and political rights of the past fifty years that has so stained the name of hospitable Ireland as this cowardly and unprovoked assassination of a friendly stranger, and that until the murderers of Lord Frederick Cavendish and Mr Burke are brought to justice that stain will sully our country's name.

Chas S. Parnell.
John Dillon.
Michael Davitt.

(*United Ireland*, 13 May 1882)

The Phoenix Park Murders. (*Le Monde Illustré*, NLI P&D)

CHAPTER VI

Home Rule

The credit for bringing the land question to the forefront belongs to Michael Davitt. However, it was Parnell who succeeded in bringing the issue to a satisfactory conclusion by means of a strategy of vigorous agitation on the ground and relentless pressure in parliament. The underlying problem of small and uneconomic holdings remained unsolved, but with the Land Act of 1881 and the Arrears Act of the following year the farmers achieved a considerable degree of security and stability. They now paid rents which were more within their means, and there was a limited scheme whereby those who were better off could buy out their farms. Tenant purchase became general after the Ashbourne Act of 1885 which Parnell was instrumental in extracting from Lord Salisbury's Conservative administration, and the social revolution leading to 'peasant proprietorship' was well and truly in train.

The people and the country derived incalculable benefit from Parnell's achievements in relation to the land. On the other hand, the agrarian campaign projected Parnell into the dominant position which he was to hold in Irish politics for a decade. He had become the 'Uncrowned King of Ireland', admired and respected by nationalists at home and abroad with the exception only of the more fanatical extremists. As a result of the agitation the nationalist population had become politicised to an unprecedented degree, and Parnell was in a position to exploit the appetite for political activity and the organisational skills developed over the previous three years. He proceeded to channel these resources into a new political organisation. He initiated the process in October 1882 by establishing the Irish National League to replace the defunct Land League.

The new organisation was effectively controlled by Parnell and the parliamentary party, and its aims were to be achieved by orthodox political activity rather than by mass agitation. Land reform was still a live issue, but the main objective was Home Rule which Parnell generally represented as amounting to the restitution of 'Grattan's Parliament'. The Irish National League was well organised on the ground and its nominees won a number of by-elections. When the franchise was extended in 1884, the political reality was that Parnell could well hold the balance of power between the Conservatives and the Liberals after the next election. That proved to be the case, and Parnell had succeeded in bringing Home Rule to the centre of the political stage at Westminster. Both parties began to show interest, but it was Gladstone and the Liberals who eventually took up the cause. In April 1886 Gladstone introduced his Home Rule Bill, but in June it was defeated by a combination of the Conservatives and a group of Liberal defectors.

However, even if Gladstone had managed to get the Home Rule Bill through the House of Commons in 1886, it would almost certainly have been vetoed by the Lords. With hindsight, it may perhaps be said that Parnell's progress was too precipitate and that he did not have enough time to market his vision of the various ways in which Home Rule could benefit both Ireland and Britain. Moreover, in the circumstances of the late seventies and the early eighties, his style of politics tended to be confrontational, and this was not conducive to wooing British opinion or to conciliating the Irish unionists.

The National League

On 17 October 1882 Parnell established the Irish National League. It replaced the Land League and included many former members. However, it was a different type of organisation and in the order of priorities land reform was secondary to Home Rule. Moreover, the new body was organised so that Parnell and the parliamentary party had effective control, and its aims were to be pursued by parliamentary action rather than by mass agitation. It attracted the support of the more conservative elements in the nationalist community, including most of the bishops. Timothy C. Harrington, MP, was secretary, and under his direction the organisation grew to the extent that within three years there were over 1,200 branches. MPs were paid from League funds, and after 1884 they were bound by a pledge to vote with the party as directed by the Whip.

An indication of Parnell's popularity in this period was the fact that at the foundation meeting of the Gaelic Athletic Association in November 1884 he was invited to become a patron along with Dr Croke, Archbishop of Cashel, and Michael Davitt. In his brief letter of acceptance, published in The Irishman on 27 December 1884, he said: 'It gives me great pleasure to learn that a Gaelic Athletic Association has been established for the preservation of national pastimes, with the objects of which I entirely concur'.

The National Conference

Yesterday the National Conference, called to deal with very important Irish questions and to establish a new national organisation, began to assemble shortly after 11 o'clock in the Antient Concert Rooms. In a short time the spacious hall was nearly filled. The assemblage included a large number of members of parliament, a considerable body of Catholic clergymen, a numerous gathering of representatives of the farming and commercial classes. ...

Mr Parnell (who was loudly cheered): Gentlemen, it now becomes my duty to put before you the programme of the constitution of the new organisation which we have decided to recommend for your adoption. ...

The proposed constitution of our organisation may be said to comprise five leading features – first, national self-government (applause); secondly, land law reform ('hear, hear'); thirdly, local self-government (applause); fourthly, extension of the parliamentary and municipal franchises (applause); and fifthly, the development and encouragement of the labour and industrial interests of Ireland. It is proposed that the name of the new organisation shall be the Irish National League ('hear, hear', and cheers). The first object of the association – of the League – is defined as the restitution to the Irish people of the right to manage their own affairs in a parliament elected by the people (cheers). I wish to re-affirm that opinion which I have expressed ever since I first stood upon an Irish platform – that until we obtain for the majority of the people of this country the right of making their own laws ('hear, hear'), we shall never be able, and we never can hope to see the laws of Ireland in accordance with the wishes of the people of Ireland ('hear, hear') – or calculated as they ought to bring about the permanent prosperity of our country ('hear, hear'). And I would always desire to impress upon my fellow-countrymen that their first duty and their first object is to obtain for our country the right of making her own laws upon Irish soil (cheers). The next branch of our constitution is that which is entitled land law reform; and, speaking for myself, I wish to re-affirm today the belief which I have expressed upon every platform upon which I have stood since the commencement of the land agitation – that no solution of the land question can be accepted as a final one that does not insure to the occupying farmers the right of becoming owners by purchase of the holdings which they now occupy as tenants (cheers). ...

(*Freeman's Journal*, 18 October 1882)

PARNELL PARTY PORTRAITS.

CHARLES S PARNELL

JUSTIN M°CARTHY.

TIMOTHY HEALY.

JOSEPH G BIGGAR.

THOMAS P O'CONNOR

THOMAS SEXTON.

JOHN E REDMOND.

CHARLES DAWSON

EDMUND D GRAY

FRANK H O'DONNELL

W™ O'BRIEN

JAMES O'KELLY

TIMOTHY D SULLIVAN.

EDMOND LEAMY.

RICHARD LALOR

JOHN DILLON

W H O'SULLIVAN

T HARRINGTON.

The 'Parnell Tribute'

Towards the end of 1882 it became known that Avondale was in financial difficulties and that Parnell was arranging to sell the estate. Many nationalists were distressed at the news and the Avoca branch of the Irish National League started a public testimonial. The scheme was promoted by the Freeman's Journal *and was strongly supported by Dr Croke, Archbishop of Cashel. Cardinal McCabe was opposed to the testimonial, and the Vatican sent a circular to the Irish bishops denouncing it. However, this had little effect and a sum of £38,000 was collected in Ireland and abroad.*

The Vatican,

Rome, May 14.

Whatever may be the case as regards Mr Parnell himself and his objects, it is at all events proved that many of his followers have on many occasions adopted a line of conduct in open contradiction to the rules laid down by the Supreme Pontiff in his letter to the Cardinal Archbishop of Dublin, and contained in the instructions sent to the Irish bishops by this Sacred Congregation, and unanimously accepted by them at their recent meeting at Dublin. ...

It is certainly not forbidden to collect for the relief of distress in Ireland; but at the same time the aforesaid apostolic mandates absolutely condemn such collections as are raised in order to inflame popular passions and to be used as the means for leading men into rebellion against the laws. Above all things they, the clergy, must hold themselves aloof from such subscriptions when it is plain that hatred and dissensions are aroused by them, that distinguished persons are loaded with insults, that never in

any way are censures pronounced against the crimes and murders with which wicked men stain themselves; and especially when it is asserted that the measure of true patriotism is in proportion to the amount of money given or refused – so as to bring the people under the pressure of intimidation.

In these circumstances, it must be evident to your lordship that the collection called the 'Parnell Testimonial Fund' cannot be approved by this Sacred Congregation; and consequently it cannot be tolerated that any ecclesiastic, much less a bishop, should take any part whatever in recommending or promoting it. Meanwhile, we pray God long to preserve your lordship.

– The text of the Vatican circular to the Irish bishops.

(*The Times,* 15 May 1883)

SUPPLEMENT TO THE WEEKLY IRISH TIMES — UNDER WHICH KING? — Saturday 26th May 1883

This cartoon from the hostile *Weekly Irish Times* illustrates the dilemma which the Vatican circular presented for Irish Catholics.

Where the Tribute went to

I have been often asked what Charley did with the sum of nearly £40,000 subscribed for him by the Irish nation. People have also wished to know how it was that, having been left by his father the fine estate of Avondale, free and unencumbered, he came to be in such straits that he had to mortgage it, and how it was that on his death, in spite of the £40,000 tribute, he was so heavily in debt. They are not easy questions to answer, but I shall endeavour to do my best.

Charley's financial embarrassment had reached a head in 1881, after returning from America. He was very anxious then to find money to send to his mother in New York as, owing to the loss of the property her brother had left her in the Black Friday panic, she was practically destitute. He wrote to me saying that, if I would mortgage my National Bank shares, he would back bills for £3,000, which I agreed to do. This shows that he had actually no money left, not even to help his own family.

Once he became leader his expenses, of course, increased enormously. A great number of the members of the Irish party had no money of their own, and he had not only to finance them in their election campaigns, but in many cases actually to keep them. So, by December 11, 1883, he was in desperate need of money. Still, he formed the resolution not to allow a penny of the £40,000 to go out of the country. I remember him telling me this, and also giving me some idea to what purposes he intended to devote the tribute money. There was a mortgage on Avondale of £5,000, which he paid off, though he afterwards remortgaged the property for £6,000. A mortgage of £10,000 in favour of our aunt, Mrs Wigram, he left outstanding, and I had finally to pay it off. On his quarries he also sank a great deal, and an attempt to develop the gold resources of the Wicklow Hills which, although a certain amount of gold was found, never paid, cost him fully £500. At the start the Arklow quarry cost him £10,000, and before it began to pay he had to spend another £5,000 on machinery. In addition, he bought up the head-rent of the Kingston demesne near Avondale for £3,000, and spent fully £1,500 in doing up Mount Avon House. He also paid off a number of debts which he had contracted in Wicklow and elsewhere. It must be remembered, of course, that the wages he was paying his men at Avondale, who were engaged in various occupations, amounted to quite £50 a week. Then, during the famine years very few of the tenants on the Avondale estate paid their rents, and even after the famine was over they kept up this custom largely, finding that he was an easy-going landlord and could not bear the idea of eviction.

You do not wonder, under these circumstances, at his occasionally showing the attitude described in the following anecdote which I believe to be perfectly true. He had addressed a crowded meeting one day in his own county of Wicklow, and was driving away to another meeting some distance off, when a friend who was with him in the car noticed one of the men who had been cheering Charley's speech most enthusiastically at the meeting, following the car with dog-like devotion mile after mile. The man kept on following, cheering and waving his hat as he went, but Charley sat upright and expressionless in the car. His friend, taking pity on so much unrequited loyalty, said to Charley: 'You might just say a word of encouragement to that poor fellow; he has followed you for seven miles and hasn't got so much as a smile from you.' 'Let him run a little longer,' said Charley, 'seeing that I have let his rent run for seven years'. ...

His debts, which I had to pay after his death, compelling me to sell Avondale, amounted to over £50,000, a figure which I have just verified. The sum total which he spent between 1881 and 1891 amounted to about £90,000. ...

The foregoing will give some idea of the many expenses which Charley had to meet, and will show that even such a sum as £40,000 could be easily swallowed up by his liabilities and current expenses.

I remember him in 1887 complaining of the financial difficulties in which he again found himself involved, and saying to me: 'Well, John, politics is the only thing I ever got any money from, and I am looking for another subscription now.' I think he was quite serious when he said it, but, of course, a fresh tribute was not forthcoming.

(J.H. Parnell, *C.S. Parnell*, pp. 286-9)

Parnell on Home Rule

The Ulster unionists regarded the campaign for Home Rule with mounting hostility. In 1884 they perceived Gladstone's proposal to broaden the franchise as a serious threat as it would reduce their virtual monopoly of power. Tension was raised when a number of nationalist MPs held meetings in the province to promote the registration of electors.

Over the years, Parnell generally represented his vision of Home Rule as the restoration of 'Grattan's Parliament'. On 21 January 1885 he reiterated this understanding of Home Rule in a famous speech in his own constituency of Cork City. His claim, 'no man has the right to fix the boundary to the march of a nation', seemed to suggest that he favoured complete independence, at least in the long term.

Later that year, Parnell formulated specific proposals for Home Rule which he outlined in his 'Proposed Constitution for Ireland'. This document was transmitted to Gladstone, who was then out of office, by Katharine O'Shea on 30 October 1885.

MR PARNELL, MP, IN CORK
Great Meeting in the Opera House

Mr Parnell: ... At the election in 1880 I laid certain principles before you, and you accepted them (applause and cries of 'we do'). I said and I pledged myself, that I should form one of an independent Irish party to act in opposition to every English government which refused to concede the just rights of Ireland (applause). And the longer time which is gone by since then, the more I am convinced that that is the true policy to pursue so far as parliamentary policy is concerned, and that it will be impossible for either or both of the English parties to contend for any long time against a determined band of Irishmen acting honestly upon these principles and backed by the Irish people (cheers). ...

Well, but gentlemen, I go back from the consideration of these questions to the land question, in which the labourers' question is also involved and the manufacturers' question. I come back, and every Irish politician must be forcibly driven back, to the consideration of the great question of national self-government for Ireland (cheers). I do not know whether England will be wise in time and concede to constitutional arguments and methods the restitution of that which was stolen from us towards the close of the last century (cheers). It is given to none of us to forecast the future, and just as it is impossible for us to say in what way or by what means the national question may be settled, in what way full justice may be done to Ireland, so it is impossible for us to say to what extent that justice should be done. We cannot ask for less than restitution of Grattan's Parliament (loud cheers), with its important privileges and wide and far-reaching constitution. We cannot under the British constitution ask for more than the restitution of Grattan's Parliament (renewed cheers), but no man has the right to fix the boundary to the march of a nation (great cheers). No man has the right to say to his country, 'thus far shalt thou go and no further,' and we have never attempted to fix the *ne plus ultra* to the progress of Ireland's nationhood, and we never shall (cheers). But, gentlemen, while we leave those things to time, circumstances and the future, we must each one of us resolve in our own hearts that we shall at all times do everything that within us lies to obtain for Ireland the fullest measure of her rights (applause). In this way we shall avoid difficulties and contentions amongst each other. In this way we shall not give up anything which the future may put in favour of our country; and while we struggle today for that which may seem possible for us with our combination, we must struggle for it with the proud consciousness that we shall not do anything to hinder or prevent better men who may come after us from gaining better things than those for which we now contend (prolonged applause).

(*Freeman's Journal*, **22 January 1885**)

A Proposed Constitution for Ireland

An elected Chamber with power to make enactments regarding all the domestic concerns of Ireland, but without power to interfere in any Imperial matter.

The Chamber to consist of three hundred members.

Two hundred and six of the number to be elected under the present suffrage, by the present Irish constituencies, with special arrangements for securing to the Protestant minority a representation proportionate to their numbers; the remaining ninety-four members to be named in the act constituting the Chamber. ...

The Chamber shall have power to enact laws and make regulations regarding all the domestic and internal affairs of Ireland, including her sea fisheries.

The Chamber shall also have power to raise a revenue for any purpose over which it has jurisdiction, by direct taxation upon property, by customs duties and by licences.

The Chamber shall have power to create departments for the transaction of all business connected with the affairs over which it has jurisdiction, and to appoint and dismiss chief and subordinate officials for such departments, to fix the term of their office, and to fix and pay their salaries; and to maintain a police force for the preservation of order and the enforcement of the law.

This power will include the constitution of Courts of Justice and the appointment and payment of all judges, magistrates, and other officials of such Courts, provided that the appointment of judges and magistrates shall in each case be subject to the assent of the Crown.

No enactment of the Chamber shall have the force of law until it shall have received the assent of the Crown. ...

The right of the Imperial Parliament to legislate regarding the domestic concerns and internal affairs of Ireland will also be held in suspense, only to be exercised for weighty and urgent cause.

The abolition of the office of Lord Lieutenant of Ireland and all other offices in Ireland under the Crown connected with the domestic affairs of that country.

The representation of Ireland in the Imperial Parliament might be retained or might be given up. If it be retained the Speaker might have power to decide what questions the Irish members might take part in as Imperial questions, if this limitation were thought desirable.

Such naval and military force as the Crown thought requisite from time to time would be maintained in Ireland out of the contribution of one million pounds per annum to the Imperial Treasury; any excess in the cost of these forces over such sum being provided for out of the Imperial revenue (i.e. by Great Britain).

– The text is the same as that of the original in the Gladstone Papers in the British Library.

(K. O'Shea, *C.S. Parnell*, ii, 18-20)

One of many posters issued by the unionists in 1884. (NLI P&D)

The 'Galway Mutiny'

In June 1885 Parnell joined forces with the Conservatives and forced the Liberals out of office. During Lord Salisbury's interim Conservative administration it was generally agreed that Parnell might well hold the balance of power after the next election. He was thus well placed to seek commitments on Home Rule from both parties. Eventually, shortly before the general election of December 1885, he authorised a manifesto calling on the Irish in Britain to support the Conservatives.

After the election, Parnell had a following of eighty-five MPs and held the balance of power. But he was immediately faced with a serious crisis in the Irish Parliamentary Party. Over the years, Captain O'Shea had gradually deserted the party and as a result failed to get nominated for an Irish constituency. Parnell put him forward for a Liverpool seat but he was rejected by the electorate. When a by-election was called for Galway, Parnell nominated him as the party candidate even though he refused to pledge himself to vote with the party. Parnell justified his action on the grounds that he would need O'Shea in the future as a channel of communication with the Liberals. O'Shea was eventually allowed to stand and was elected in due course, but the loyalty of some of Parnell's most faithful followers was severely strained.

Manifesto to the Irish Electors in Great Britain
To our Countrymen in England and Scotland

...In no case ought an Irish nationalist to give a vote, in our opinion, to a member of that Liberal or Radical party except in some few cases in which courageous fealty to the Irish cause in the last Parliament has given a guarantee that the candidate will not belong to the servile, and cowardly, and unprincipled herd that would break every pledge and violate every principle in obedience to the call of the Whip and the mandate to the caucus. The Executive of the National League will communicate the names of the candidates who they think would be excepted from the terms of this manifesto. In every other instance we earnestly advise our countrymen to vote against the men who coerced Ireland, deluged Egypt with blood, menaced religious liberty in the school, freedom of speech in Parliament, and promised to the country generally a repetition of the crimes and follies of the last Liberal Administration.

(Signed) T.P. O'Connor, President of the Irish National League of Great Britain

Justin M'Carthy }	
Thos Sexton }	
T.M. Healy }	Executive
J.E. Redmond }	
James O'Kelly }	
J.G. Biggar }	

(*The Nation,* 28 November 1885)

'THE GENERAL ELECTION GAME: THE IRISH CHIEF HAS JUST DEALT THE CARDS' – Parnell with Lord Randolph Churchill and Lord Salisbury on his right, and Gladstone and Joseph Chamberlain on his left.

Parnell's dominating personality

It was announced that there was a meeting waiting for us which we were expected to address. I have always regarded the proceedings of that meeting as bringing out more than almost any other incident in his life the tremendous courage and the dominating personality of Parnell. Yet, there was nothing in the outward appearance of the meeting to bring out its tremendous importance. It was held in a small, rickety hall bearing palpable evidence of what was, alas! the universal feature of Galway life at that time – pretentious and hopeful beginning and gradual and despairing decay. Except for a few chairs on a small platform, there was not any sitting accommodation; the howling mob was there, standing, fierce, impatient.

I took the chair and got a rather mixed reception. And then Parnell spoke. I need not elaborate on the desperate issues he was fighting; on the essential and indefensible weakness of his position; on the terrible case, if all the truth were known, he had to meet and that on the direct issue it was impossible for him to meet. Parnell, as I have more than once remarked, was usually rather a poor speaker – hesitating, costive, with unimpressive, lame sentences; but with his back to the wall now, he showed that on occasion he could rise to heights of irresistible appeal. I do not remember that he ever even mentioned the name of Captain O'Shea; he gave a complete go-by both to the attacks that had been made upon that gentleman personally or to the replies that might be made. He did not repeat to them the palpably insincere claims of O'Shea's services to the cause which he had uttered in that momentous interview between him and me outside the House of Commons. The passage which swept away the audience and won the day was, so far as I can repeat the words, in something like these terms. Lifting his arm and stretching out his hand, he said: 'I have Home Rule for Ireland in the hollow of my hand. If you dispute my decision now the English will say, "Parnell's power is broken"; and that will be the end of the Home Rule Movement.'

You could almost feel the shudder of terror and of subjugation which swept through the audience, brought back from its howling fury to the sepulchral silence of a death-chamber.

– The meeting took place on 9 February 1886.

(T.P. O'Connor, *Memoirs of an Old Parliamentarian*, pp. 102-3)

Telegram from three MPs to William O'Brien in support of Parnell, 9 February 1886. (NLI MS 5385)

The Irish Parliamentary Party, April 1886

1. J. Stack (North Kerry)
2. W.M. Murphy (Dublin City, St Patrick's)
3. Dr J.E. Kenny (Cork County, South)
4. Jeremiah Jordan (West Clare)
5. J.R. Cox (East Clare)
6. E. Dwyer Gray (Dublin City, Harbour)
7. Bernard Kelly (South Donegal)
8. W.J. Lane (Cork County)
9. P.J. O'Brien (North Tipperary)
10. P.A. Chance (South Kilkenny)
11. Timothy M. Healy (North Monaghan)
12. J.M. Smithwick (Kilkenny City)
13. W.J. Corbett (East Wicklow)
14. P.J. Power (East Waterford)
15. L.P. Hayden (South Waterford)
16. Maurice Healy (Cork City)
17.

18. Sir J.W. McKenna (South Monaghan)
19. A. Blaine (South Armagh)
20. J.C. Flynn (Cork County, North)
21. T.P. Gill (South Louth)
22. J. Barry (South Wexford)
23. P.R. Condon (East Tipperary)
24. Joseph Biggar (West Cavan)
25. E. Sheil (South Meath)
26. W. Abraham (West Limerick)
27. Joseph Nolan (North Longford)
28. L. Connolly (South Longford)
29. Matthew Harris (East Galway)
30. Dr Andrew Commins (South Roscommon)
31. Dr Kevin Izod O'Doherty (North Meath)
32. D. Crilly (South Mayo)
33. P. Sheehan (East Kerry)
34. J.F.X. O'Brien (South Mayo)
35. E.M. Marum (North Kilkenny)

36. J. Leahy (South Kildare)
37. Garrett Byrne (West Kerry)
38. Edward Harrington (West Kerry)
39. M.J. Kenny (Mid Tyrone)
40. T.P. O'Connor (Liverpool, Scotland Ward)
41. M. Conway (North Leitrim)
42. T.M. Carew (North Kildare)
43. J.F. Small (South Downshire)
44. Bernard Molloy (King's County, Birr)
45. Dr Kevin Izod O'Doherty (North Meath)
46. R. Lalor (Queen's County)
47. J.J. Clancy (Dublin County, North)
48. Arthur O'Connor (East Donegal)
49. Donal Sullivan (South Westmeath)
50. Justin Huntly McCarthy (Newry)
51. Thomas Sexton (South Sligo)
52.

53. James Tuite (North Westmeath)
54. Dr J. Fox (King's County, Tullamore)
55. James E. O'Doherty (North Donegal)
56. John Finucane (East Limerick)
57. H.J. Gill (Limerick City)
58. Major J.P. Nolan (North Galway)
59. Patrick O'Hea (West Donegal)
60. W.J. Reynolds (East Tyrone)
61. Justin McCarthy (North Longford)
62. John Deasy (West Mayo)
63. CHARLES STEWART PARNELL (Cork City)
64. W. Redmond (North Fermanagh)
65. T. Harrington (Dublin City, St Stephen's Green)
66. H. Campbell (South Fermanagh)
67. J.J. O'Kelly (North Roscommon)

68. P.J. Foley (Galway, Connemara)
69. Jasper D. Pyne (West Waterford)
70. Sir T.G. Esmonde, Bart (Dublin County, South)
71. David Sheehy (South Galway)
72. T. Mayne (Mid Tipperary)
73. John O'Connor (South Kerry)
74. Peter McDonald (North Sligo)
75. John Dillon (East Mayo)
76. Richard Power (Waterford City)
77. J.E. Redmond (North West Cork)
78. Timothy Daniel Sullivan (Dublin City, College Green, Lord Mayor)
79. W. O'Brien (South Tyrone)
80. T. O'Hanlon (East Cavan)

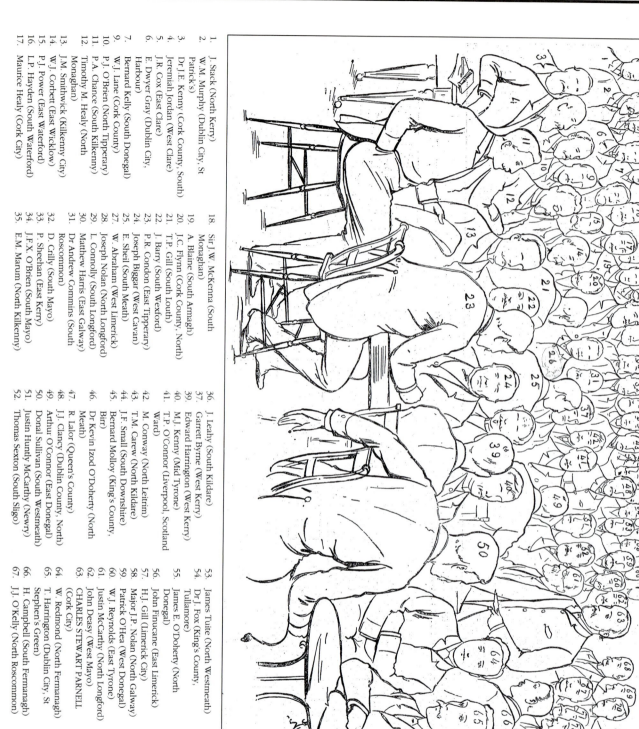

(Illustrated London News, 10 April 1886)

67

Gladstone's Home Rule Bill

On 8 April 1886 Gladstone introduced his Home Rule Bill. It provided for an Irish parliament with upper and lower chambers and an executive. Matters of imperial concern were to remain the responsibility of the United Kingdom parliament, but Ireland would no longer have representation there. Parnell regarded the Bill as inadequate but he supported it in the belief that it could provide the basis for further progress. It caused a split in the Liberal party, and Joseph Chamberlain and ninety other Liberals, thereafter known as Liberal Unionists, voted against the Bill. It was defeated by 341 to 311 votes.

The Parnell of the Home Rule Bill

It was on a raw February night during the recess he made the announcement to four or five of us in his sitting-room at Morrison's Hotel, in Dublin. With his characteristic indifference to personal discomfort, he had neglected to order a fire, and his mutton cutlet was growing cold and his pint of Rhine wine unopened, while he doggedly made his way through bundle after bundle of letters awaiting his arrival. All of a sudden the very room lighted up for some of us like a bit of heaven when, raising his head from some dull document, concerning God knows what, in which he had been absorbed, he remarked casually and without emphasis: 'We are going to have a Home Rule Bill. Will you, gentlemen, kindly turn it over and let me have your suggestions as to what we want – I mean, what we can get?' The youth of a more fortunate time will never understand the flow of incredulous rapture the words sent through every fibre of one like myself who had entered upon the *via dolorosa* of the nationalist struggle with an all but fatalist persuasion that it was bound to end in failure, desperation, penal servitude, or the gallows.

(W. O'Brien, *Parnell*, pp. 106-7)

		J.E.Redmond				T.D. Sullivan			John Fitzgerald
J.B. O'Reilly	John Barry				T.M. Healy	Michael Davitt	T.P. O'Connor	T.Brennan	Timothy Harrington
E.D. Gray	John Ferguson	Patrick Egan		Professor Galbraith	Archbishop Walsh			Sir T. Esmonde	
General P.A. Collins	Alexander Sullivan					Archbishop Croke			
Justin McCarthy	John Dillon		Charles Stewart Parnell				Thomas Sexton	Joseph G. Biggar	William O'Brien

'IRISH NATIONALIST PARTY UNDER CHARLES STEWART PARNELL'. A print from a composite painting by W. Drummond Young which is now in the House of Commons in London. It is set in the former Irish House of Commons and includes those who contributed most to the Home Rule movement. (NLI P&D)

W P SWAN LITH

DUBLIN

W. E. GLADSTONE moving the Second Reading of the Home Rule Bill.

House of Commons, May 10th, 1886.

Parnell is in the second row on the right; to his left are Tim Healy, T.P. O'Connor, John Redmond and J.G. Biggar.

Nationalists

MPs Elected July 1886

(By W.T. Parkes)

CHAPTER VII

The Special Commission

In the general election in July 1886 following the defeat of the Home Rule Bill, the Irish party secured eighty-five seats, just one less than on the previous occasion. Gladstone and the Liberals lost much of their support, and the Conservatives formed the new government with Lord Salisbury as Prime Minister. For the next four years Parnell remained firmly committed to the Liberals, and he seemed confident that they would deliver Home Rule when they returned to power. In the meantime, he concentrated on parliamentary action, and he was not in favour of the Plan of Campaign which began in October 1886. Indeed, in the latter part of that year and throughout the following year his political contribution was drastically reduced as he was obviously in poor health. He attended Sir Henry Thompson, a London urologist, but there is no convincing evidence of a serious kidney ailment. The ill-health and exhaustion at that time may have been due to stress.

It was in these circumstances that he was confronted with one of the most serious threats of his career. It arose in the spring of 1887 with the publication in *The Times* of a series of articles entitled 'Parnellism and Crime'.The claim was made that during the land agitation of 1879-82 Parnell and a number of his close associates had promoted crime and civil disorder, and that they conspired to effect the complete separation of Ireland from Britain. *The Times* also published the facsimile of a letter alleged to have been written by Parnell in May 1882 in which he seemed to apologise for denouncing the Phoenix Park murders.

The government made the most of the opportunity to damage Parnell and the Home Rule movement. In August 1888 it established a Special Commission to investigate the allegations. In effect, Parnell, Michael Davitt, and sixty-four former and current MPs were put on trial before a tribunal of three judges. *The Times* had the responsibility of substantiating its allegations and it acted more or less as a prosecution. The government did its best to influence the outcome, and it coerced the Attorney-General, Sir Richard Webster, into acting as counsel for *The Times*. It also gave the lawyers representing *The Times* access to official files relating to the Land League and the Fenians. This action was authorised by the Chief Secretary for Ireland, Arthur Balfour, who, incidentally, was a nephew of Lord Salisbury. Among the witnesses for *The Times* was the government spy, Henri Le Caron, who did his best to incriminate Parnell.

In the course of the inquiry it transpired that the articles in *The Times* were the result of a plot by the Irish Loyal and Patriotic Union. The Union's secretary, Edward Caulfield Houston, had hired Richard Pigott, a former Fenian, to find evidence to incriminate Parnell. Pigott happened to have copies of Parnell's signature as he had dealings with him in 1881 when *United Ireland* was being planned and he had sold him *The Irishman* and two other newspapers. In due course, Pigott presented letters which suggested that Parnell was involved with subversives. Houston bought them and passed them on to *The Times*. However, in the course of the enquiry it became apparent that Pigott had actually forged the letters.

'Parnellism and Crime'

The first article in the series, 'Parnellism and Crime', appeared in The Times *on 7 March 1887. Allegations that Parnell was involved with extremists had become common over the years and the articles did not attract much attention. However, on 18 April* The Times *published a facsimile of a letter which it claimed was written by Parnell in May 1882, shortly after the Phoenix Park murders. The letter was supposed to be addressed to Patrick Egan, a known Fenian and former secretary of the Land League. The text of the letter was obviously not in Parnell's hand, but the conclusion, 'Yours very truly,' and the signature, certainly resembled his handwriting.* The Times *had a reputation for reliability and many people, especially in England, accepted the letter as genuine. The implication that Parnell was not sincere when he denounced the Phoenix Park murders was extremely damaging.*

The night the letter was published Parnell made a statement in the House of Commons disclaiming responsibility for it and denying any knowledge of the Invincibles' conspiracy before the murders took place. He referred to the former Chief Secretary, W.E. Forster, as it was generally believed that he, rather than Lord Frederick Cavendish, was the assassins' principal target. In 1882 the main political result of the murders was that the country had to endure another period of coercion.

PARNELLISM AND CRIME
Mr Parnell and the Phoenix Park Murders

In concluding our series of articles on 'Parnellism and Crime', we intimated that, besides the damning facts which we there recorded, unpublished evidence existed which would bind still closer the links between the 'constitutional' chiefs and the contrivers of murder and outrage. In view of the unblushing denials of Mr Sexton and Mr Healy on Friday night, we do not think it right to withhold any longer from public knowledge the fact that we possess and have had in our custody for some time documentary evidence which has a most serious bearing on the Parnellite conspiracy and which, after a most careful and minute scrutiny, is, we are satisfied, quite authentic. We produce one document in facsimile today by a process the accuracy of which cannot be impugned, and we invite Mr Parnell to explain how his signature has become attached to such a letter.

It is requisite to point out that the body of the manuscript is apparently not in Mr Parnell's handwriting, but the signature and the 'Yours very truly' unquestionably are so; and if any Member of Parliament doubts the fact, he can easily satisfy himself on the matter by comparing the handwriting with that of Mr Parnell in the book containing the signature of members when they first take their seats in the House of Commons.

The body of the letter occupies the whole of the first page of an ordinary sheet of stout white note-paper, leaving no room in the same page for the signature which is placed on the fourth page near the top right-hand corner. It was an obvious precaution to sign upon the back instead of upon the second page, so that the half-sheet might if necessary be torn off and the letter disclaimed.

It is right and necessary to explain that the 'Dear Sir' is believed to be Egan and that the letter was addressed to him in order to pacify the wrath of his subordinate instruments in the Phoenix Park murders – then (on May 15, nine days after the tragedy) still at large and undetected. The anxiety of the writer to keep his address unknown will be noted and is curious in connexion with a belief prevailing at the time that Mr Parnell was so impressed by the danger he had incurred by denouncing the assassinations as to have applied for the protection of the police on the plea that his life was in peril.

(*The Times*, 18 April 1887)

Mr Parnell... But when I saw what purported to be my signature, I saw plainly that it was an audacious and unblushing fabrication. Why, Sir, many Members of this House have seen my signature, and if they will compare it with what purports to be my signature in *The Times* of this morning, they will see that there are only two letters in the whole name which bear any resemblance to letters in my own signature as I write it. I cannot understand how the conductors of a responsible, and what used to be a respectable, journal could have been so hoodwinked, so hoaxed, so bamboozled, and that is the most charitable interpretation which I can place on it, as to publish such a production as that as my signature. ...

I think I should insult myself if I said – I think, however, that I perhaps ought to say it in order that my denial may be full and complete – that I certainly never heard of the letter. I never directed such a letter to be written. I never saw such a letter before I saw it in *The Times* this morning. The subject-matter of the letter is preposterous on the surface. The phraseology of it is absurd – as absurd as any phraseology that could be attributed to me could possibly be. In every part of it, it bears absolute and irrefutable evidence of want of genuineness and want of authenticity. Politics are come to a pretty pass in this country when a Leader of a Party of 86 Members has to stand up, at ten minutes past one, in the House of Commons in order to defend himself from an anonymous fabrication such as that which is contained in *The Times* this morning. I have always held, with regard to the late Mr Forster, that his treatment of his political prisoners was a humane treatment and a fair treatment, and I think for that reason alone, if for no other, he should have been shielded from such an attempt as was made on his life by the Invincible Association. I never had the slightest notion in the world that the life of the late Mr Forster was in danger, or that any conspiracy was on foot against him or any other official in Ireland or elsewhere. I had no more notion than an unborn child that there was such a conspiracy as that of the Invincibles in existence, and no one was more surprised, more thunderstruck, and more astonished than I was when that bolt from the blue fell upon us in the Phoenix Park murders. I knew not in what direction to look for this calamity. It is no exaggeration to say that if I had been in the Park that day, I would gladly have stood between Lord Frederick Cavendish and the daggers of the assassins, and for the matter of that between their daggers and Mr Burke too. Now, Sir, I leave this subject. I have suffered more than any other man from that terrible deed in the Phoenix Park, and the Irish nation has suffered more than any other nation through it.

(Hansard, Parliamentary Debates, 18 April 1887, 1226-8)

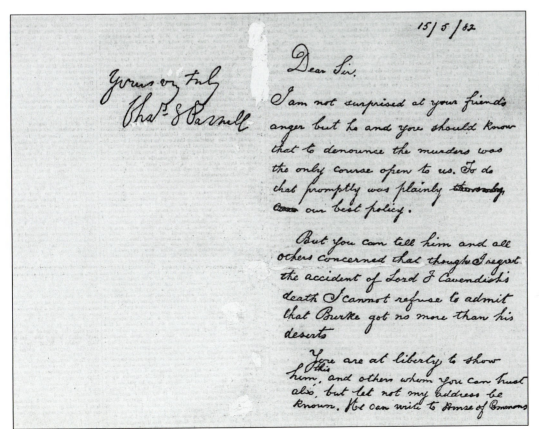

The letter published in *The Times,* 18 April 1887.

The Players

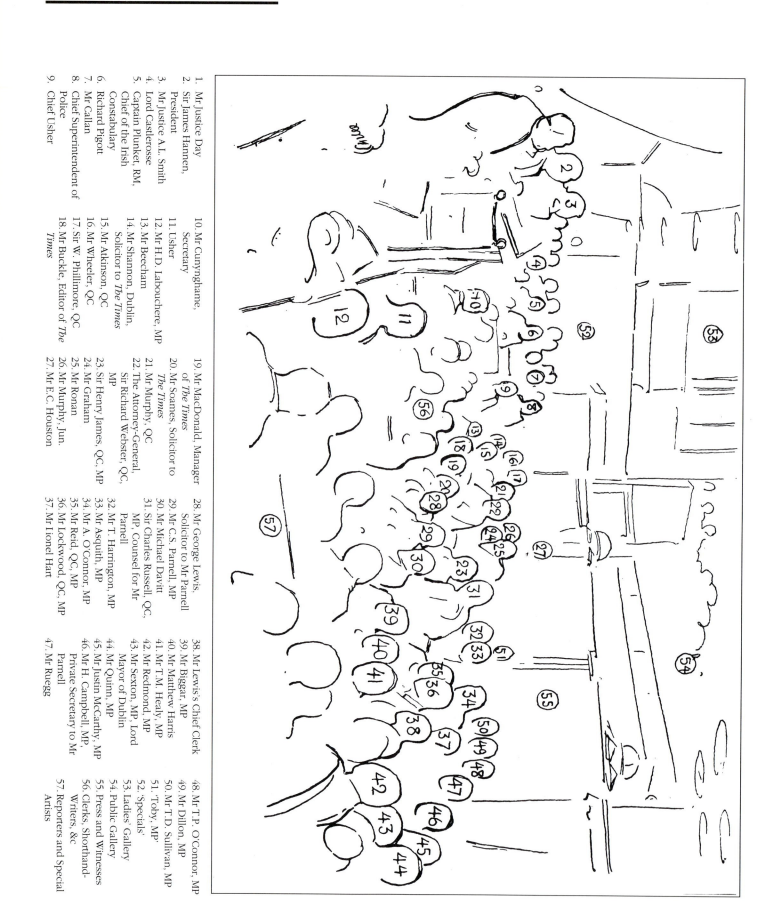

1. Mr Justice Day
2. Sir James Hannen, President
3. Mr Justice A.L. Smith
4. Lord Castlerosse
5. Captain Plunket, RM, Chief of the Irish Constabulary
6. Richard Pigott
7. Mr Callan
8. Chief Superintendent of Police
9. Chief Usher
10. Mr Cunynghame, Secretary
11. Usher
12. Mr H.D. Labouchere, MP
13. Mr Beecham
14. Mr Shannon, Dublin, Solicitor to *The Times*
15. Mr Atkinson, QC
16. Mr Wheeler, QC
17. Sir W. Phillimore, QC
18. Mr Buckle, Editor of *The Times*
19. Mr MacDonald, Manager of *The Times*
20. Mr Soames, Solicitor to *The Times*
21. Mr Murphy, QC
22. The Attorney-General, Sir Richard Webster, QC, MP
23. Sir Henry James, QC, MP
24. Mr Graham
25. Mr Ronan
26. Mr Murphy, Jun.
27. Mr E.C. Houston
28. Mr George Lewis, Solicitor to Mr Parnell
29. Mr C.S. Parnell, MP
30. Mr Michael Davitt
31. Sir Charles Russell, QC, MP, Counsel for Mr Parnell
32. Mr T. Harrington, MP
33. Mr Asquith, MP
34. Mr A. O'Connor, MP
35. Mr Reid, QC, MP
36. Mr Lockwood, QC, MP
37. Mr Lionel Hart
38. Mr Lewis's Chief Clerk
39. Mr Biggar, MP
40. Mr Matthew Harris
41. Mr T.M. Healy, MP
42. Mr Redmond, MP
43. Mr Sexton, MP, Lord Mayor of Dublin
44. Mr Quinn, MP
45. Mr Justin McCarthy, MP
46. Mr H. Campbell, MP, Private Secretary to Mr Parnell
47. Mr Ruegg
48. Mr T.P. O'Connor, MP
49. Mr Dillon, MP
50. Mr T.D. Sullivan, MP
51. 'Toby, MP'
52. 'Specials'
53. Ladies' Gallery
54. Public Gallery
55. Press and Witnesses
56. Clerks, Shorthand-Writers, &c
57. Reporters and Special Artists

'THE SPECIAL COMMISSION', by Thomas Walter Wilson. (*Illustrated London News*, 9 March 1889)

75

The Letters

Richard Pigott hoped to make money out of both parties in the affair. After he sold his forged letters to Edward Caulfield Houston, he offered his services to the Parnellites to defeat the impending plot. He tried to use Dr Walsh, Archbishop of Dublin, as an intermediary, but Dr Walsh was suspicious and returned all but one of his letters. Pigott thought he had got all the letters back, and in his evidence to the Special Commission he blithely swore that he did not know that The Times *was about to publish allegations against Parnell until the first article appeared on 7 March 1887. When Parnell's counsel, Sir Charles Russell, confronted him with his letter of 4 March to Dr Walsh, his duplicity became apparent.*

In the course of the Special Commission, The Times *submitted a letter alleged to be in the hand of Parnell's secretary, Henry Campbell, but signed by himself. It was supposed to have been written in January 1881, when Parnell was in prison in Kilmainham, and to be addressed to Patrick Egan who was in Paris at that time. It had two spelling mistakes, and when Sir Charles Russell asked Pigott to write the word 'hesitancy', he mis-spelled it as in the letter.*

My Lord,

The importance of the matter about which I write will doubtless excuse this intrusion on your Grace's attention.

Briefly, I wish to say that I have been made aware of the details of certain proceedings that are in preparation with the object of destroying the influence of the Parnellite party in Parliament.

I cannot enter more fully into details than to state that the proceedings referred to consist in the publication of certain statements purporting to prove the complicity of Mr Parnell himself and some of his supporters with murder and outrages in Ireland, to be followed in all probability by the institution of criminal proceedings against these parties by the government.

Your Grace may be assured that I speak with full knowledge and am in a position to prove, beyond all doubt or question, the truth of what I say. And I could further assure your Grace that I am also able to point out how the design may be successfully com-

batted [*sic*] and finally defeated. I assure your Grace that I have no other motive except to respectfully suggest that your Grace would communicate the substance of what I state to some one or other of the parties concerned – on, however, the specific understanding that my name will be kept secret – to whom I could furnish details, exhibit proofs, and suggest how the coming blow may be effectively met. ...

I remain,
With humble respect,
Your Grace's obedient humble servant,
Richard Pigott.

(Dublin Diocesan Archives, Archbishop Walsh Papers)

Drawing by Frederick Pegram. (*The Parnell Commission* [1890], p. 25)

Drawing by Frederick Pegram. (*The Parnell Commission* [1890], p. 25)

9/1/82

Dear E.

What are these fellows waiting for? This inaction is inexcusable. Our best men are in prison and nothing is being done.

Let there be an end of this hesitency Prompt action is called for.

You undertook to make it hot for old Forster and Co. Let us have some evidence of your power to do so.

My health is good thanks

Yours very truly
Chas S Parnell

A facsimile of one of the forged letters. (NLI P&D)

Drawing by Sydney Prior Hall of Parnell in the witness-box with Archbishop Walsh behind him. (*Daily Graphic*, Supplement, 6 December 1890)

The Story

The Parnell Inquiry Commission

After evidence given by Mr MacDonald, the manager of *The Times,* Mr Edward Caulfield Houston, a journalist who is secretary to the Irish Loyal and Patriotic Union, was called as a witness by the Attorney-General. He stated that Mr Richard Pigott, formerly editor and proprietor of *The Irishman,* who had furnished him with materials for a pamphlet called 'Parnellism Unmasked' in March or April 1886, got the letters for him which he said had been left in a bag at Paris. Mr Houston borrowed some money and paid Mr Pigott £1,250 for the letters; he also provided for the expenses of Mr Pigott's journeys to Paris, to Lausanne and to New York. In June or July 1887 he put himself in communication with Mr MacDonald, and *The Times* ultimately purchased the letters from Mr Houston, paying for them £2,530 in all, these transactions going on till the early part of 1888. Mr Houston was cross-examined by Sir Charles Russell, and stated that he had, since this judicial inquiry began, destroyed most of the documents belonging to his correspondence with Mr Pigott, explaining that his reason for so doing was to save Mr Pigott from being compromised with the persons from whom he obtained those letters.

The next witness called was Mr Pigott himself, who admitted having been since 1865 a Fenian and one of the Irish Republican Brotherhood; but ceased attending it when he gave up his paper in July 1881 and sold his paper to the Land League. In 1885 he wrote a pamphlet against the Parnellites and formed a connection with Mr Houston, undertaking to procure documents for the exposure of their conspiracy; he was to be paid a guinea a day and his travelling expenses. Mr Pigott, early in 1886, twice went to Lausanne to confer with a Mr Eugene Davis there, who had been intimately conversant with the Land League in Ireland. Soon afterwards, in April, he met in Paris one Maurice Murphy, formerly a compositor in the office of *The Irishman* and an agent of the American Clan na Gael. This man told him of the bag containing eleven of Mr Parnell's and Mr Egan's letters, and wanted £1,000 for getting them, but agreed to take £500; and as the Clan na Gael had a claim on them, Mr Pigott went to America to obtain authority for their being handed over to him. He was obliged to take an oath never to reveal the manner in which they came into his possession. He received from Mr Houston £100 as commission, besides the £500 he had paid for them, and his expenses and daily stipend for many months.

In the latter months of 1888, when the Commission of Inquiry was opened, he was in communication with Mr Labouchere and with Mr George Lewis, solicitor for Mr Parnell, respecting the evidence which he should give concerning the letters which those gentlemen denounced as forgeries of his own. He said that Mr Labouchere, on October 26, 1888, offered him £1,000 to confess that they were forgeries; but this statement was not corroborated by a number of subsequent letters of Mr Labouchere, who only sent him £10 for the expenses of a journey between Dublin and London.

Mr Pigott was severely cross-examined with reference to his correspondence in 1887 with Archbishop Walsh, offering to combat and defeat the charges against Mr Parnell; and with regard also to his applications to the late Right Hon. W.E. Forster in 1881, begging for money and professing his readiness to write against the Land League when he found that Mr Parnell would not promise him continued employment on *The Irishman.* The admissions he was forced to make were tacitly compared with what Mr Houston had deemed his straightforward conduct in dealing with the alleged Parnell letters. On Tuesday, February 26, when the Court sat again, Mr Pigott did not appear, having left his hotel the night before, and a warrant was issued for his apprehension at the request of Sir Charles Russell, with orders to seize a number of letters left for him at the hotel.

(*Illustrated London News,* 2 March 1889)

THE ILLUSTRATED LONDON NEWS

No. 2612.—VOL. XCIV.　　　SATURDAY, MAY 11, 1889.　　　TWO WHOLE SHEETS AND EXTRA SUPPLEMENT } SIXPENCE. By Post, 6½p.

Parnell in the witness-box, by R. Taylor.

Parnell Vindicated

Pigott made a statement admitting he forged the letters. He then fled to Madrid where he committed suicide. Although the Commission continued until February 1890, the exposure of the forgery exonerated Parnell as far as the general public was concerned. The Special Commission issued its report in February 1890. While it found that Parnell had engaged in intimidation and other questionable practices, it acquitted him of the more serious charges.

Gladstone and the Liberals had believed in Parnell's innocence throughout and maintained contact with him on the issue of Home Rule. In December 1889, Parnell visited Gladstone at Hawarden, his home in north Wales, to discuss Home Rule. The meeting was well publicised and was generally regarded as an indication that Parnell was once again a major political force.

Conclusions

I. We find that the respondent Members of Parliament collectively were not members of a conspiracy having for its object to establish the absolute independence of Ireland, but we find that some of them, together with Mr Davitt, established and joined in the Land League organisation with the intention by its means to bring about the absolute independence of Ireland as a separate nation. ...

III. We find that the charge that, 'when on certain occasions they thought it politic to denounce, and did denounce certain crimes in public they afterwards led their supporters to believe such denunciations were not sincere', is not established. We entirely acquit Mr Parnell and the other respondents of the charge of insincerity in their denunciation of the Phoenix Park murders, and find that the 'facsimile' letter on which this charge was chiefly based as against Mr Parnell is a forgery.

(*Report of the Special Commission*, p. 119)

SUPPLEMENT GIVEN AWAY WITH THE **WEEKLY FREEMAN** 28TH DECEMBER, 1889.   PRICE THREE HALF-PENCE

WELCOME TO HAWARDEN

IRISH AFFAIRS

"GOOD HEALTH!"

CHAPTER VIII

The Split

In Ireland there was great rejoicing that Parnell had succeeded in confounding *The Times,* the unionists and the government. At the time political prospects seemed very favourable from the nationalist point of view, as the Conservatives' term of office was coming towards the end, and the Liberals were expected to form the next government. Following the Hawarden meeting with Gladstone, Parnell seemed confident that the Liberals could be trusted to force Home Rule through at the second attempt.

It was then, when circumstances seemed most auspicious, that disaster struck. For ten years Parnell had lived almost continually with Katharine O'Shea at her home in Eltham. While they managed to keep the affair from the public at large, her husband and many other people were aware of it from an early stage. For purely selfish motives Captain O'Shea let the situation continue unchecked over the years, but by the end of 1889 circumstances had changed. As he had resigned his seat in parliament, Parnell was no longer of any use to him for political purposes. Also, it had turned out that he was not entitled to a share in Katharine's legacy from her Aunt Ben. In any case, ten days after the Hawarden meeting he filed for divorce on the grounds of his wife's adultery with Parnell.

Many people presumed that the accusation was just another unionist plot, and Parnell claimed that the trial would vindicate his reputation. However, what he meant was that while the charge of adultery was technically correct, he was morally justified in his behaviour as O'Shea had deserted his wife several years before the affair began. Also, he may have hoped to settle with O'Shea but that did not prove possible. Then, when the case came to trial in November 1890, he decided that Katharine should not offer a defence as he wanted the divorce to go through so that she would be free to marry him.

Notwithstanding the hostile reaction of many nationalists, Parnell's stature was such that his continued leadership of the parliamentary party would probably not have been seriously jeopardised by the divorce scandal on its own. He had succeeded in convincing the parliamentary party and the public at large that he could deliver Home Rule, and the pragmatic view was that qualms about his private life should not be allowed to hinder the process. However, it was believed that Home Rule could only be achieved through the alliance with the Liberals. When Gladstone made it clear that the alliance could not succeed in its objective if Parnell remained leader of the Irish party, both the party and the people re-assessed the situation, and in both cases the majority view was that Parnell should resign from the leadership.

When Parnell tried to retrieve his position by belatedly claiming that Gladstone's Home Rule proposals were inadequate and that the alliance with the Liberals should be abandoned, his new tack was generally perceived as a discreditable ploy.

The Divorce

In December 1889 Captain O'Shea filed a petition for divorce on the grounds of his wife's adultery with Parnell. Parnell claimed that Edward Caulfield Houston and The Times *were behind the move and that the trial would vindicate his good name. This was generally taken to mean that he was not guilty of the adultery. However, what he meant was that he was morally justified in entering into a relationship with Mrs O'Shea as her husband had deserted her and had tacitly consented to the relationship for personal gain. Also, at that stage he probably hoped that he and Katharine could 'square' O'Shea. But that did not prove possible because neither of them had the money to buy him off, as Aunt Ben's will was contested and Katharine's legacy was held up.*

When he failed to settle with O'Shea, Parnell did not allow Katharine to contest the case so that the divorce would go through and she would become free to marry him. The result was that O'Shea was granted a decree nisi *and was given custody of the younger children, including Clare and Katharine who were Parnell's daughters. As the case was not contested, O'Shea's counsel was free to present dubious evidence of an unsavoury nature. For instance, a cook named Caroline Pethers alleged that on occasions when O'Shea turned up at a house in Brighton where Mrs O'Shea and 'Mr Stewart' were staying, 'Mr Stewart' resorted to the stratagem of escaping via the fire-escape and then appearing at the front door as if he had just arrived.*

A petition for divorce has been filed by William Henry O'Shea, of 124 Victoria Street, Westminster, and Justice of the Peace in County Clare, against his wife – Mr Charles Stewart Parnell, MP, being the co-respondent. The grounds alleged are the adultery of Mrs O'Shea during the period from April 1887 up to the date of the petition, at the undermentioned places – Eltham, 34 York Terrace, Regent's Park, Brighton, and Aldington, Sussex. No damages are claimed.

(*Evening News and Post*, **28 December 1889**)

Letter from Parnell to T.P. Gill, MP for South Louth. (NLI MS 13,506)

MR PARNELL AGAIN ASSAILED
Captain O'Shea, Houston, and *The Times*
Statement by Mr Parnell

(From our Special Correspondent)

London, Sunday Night.

I obtained an interview from Mr Parnell today with reference to the announcement of proceedings by Captain O'Shea against him in the Divorce Court. Mr Parnell stated that he had not heard up to then that any such proceedings had been taken, but said that Captain O'Shea had been threatening such proceedings for years past, in fact since 1886, when Captain O'Shea had separated himself politically from him. Mr Parnell added that he had received reliable information that Captain O'Shea had been incited for some time past to take action of this nature by Mr Edward Caulfield Houston, the hirer of Pigott, and he believes O'Shea has been induced to take these proceedings by Houston in the interests of *The Times,* in order to try and diminish the damages likely to be given in the forthcoming libel action. Mr Parnell also said that he had constantly resided at Mrs O'Shea's house at Eltham from the end of 1880 to 1886. Captain O'Shea was always aware that he (Mr Parnell) was constantly there in his (Captain O'Shea's) absence during that period, and since 1886 he has known that Mr Parnell constantly resided there from 1880 to 1886. Mr Parnell is therefore convinced that this extraordinary action on O'Shea's part is entirely in the interest of *The Times.*

(*Freeman's Journal,* 30 December 1889)

'The O'Shea - Parnell case: Sketches in court'. (*Charles Stewart Parnell* [*Daily Graphic* Pamphlets I], p. 25)

Reaction to the Divorce

Reaction to the disclosures in the divorce court was mixed. At a meeting at the Leinster Hall, Dublin, on 20 November, various prominent members of the Irish Parliamentary Party took a pragmatic view and a resolution supporting Parnell was unanimously passed. However, many of Parnell's traditional allies were seriously disturbed. For instance, Archbishop Croke felt that Parnell should resign the leadership of the party, and he believed that members of the party had been precipitate in their public declarations of loyalty.

'Sketches at the meeting at Leinster Hall'. (*Charles Stewart Parnell* [*Daily Graphic* Pamphlets I], p. 32)

The Palace, Thurles.

November 22.

My Dear Archbishop,

I do not go as far as Cardinal Manning who seems to think that Parnell's holding on to the leadership means ruin. But, I believe that by doing so he will do serious damage to the cause. Besides, if he had an atom of shame left in his composition, or if he were capable at all of gauging the situation, even from a personal point of view, he could not fail to see that retirement on Tuesday morning last would have created sympathy for him on all sides and caused a strong turn of the tide in his favour.

I do not know how he can face the House of Commons next week. Will he be hissed? or what is likely to happen?

I have flung him away from me for ever. His bust which for some time has held a prominent place in my hall I kicked out yesterday. As for the 'party' generally, I go with you entirely in thinking that they make small or no account of Bishops and priests now as independent agents, and only value them as money gatherers and useful auxiliaries in the agitation.

This I have noticed for a considerable time past; and I believe we shall have to let them see and feel unmistakably that, without us, they would simply be nowhere and nobodies. The main point at issue now is as difficult as it is a delicate one. Its difficulty is generally enhanced by the action of the press and of the Irish parliamentary party. Had silence been observed up to this, something might have been done to facilitate or bring about a reasonable compromise such as the abstention from the House of Parnell for a month or so or for all the present session.

But now, really, I fear things might be allowed to take the direction given to them by the Irish members – come what may I see no practical way out of the difficulty. ...

Yours most faithfully,
T.W. Croke.

– Letter of Dr Croke, Archbishop of Cashel, to Dr Walsh, Archbishop of Dublin.

(Dublin Diocesan Archives, Archbishop Walsh Papers)

Telegram to T.P. O'Connor who was in the United States on a fund-raising campaign when the divorce took place. (NLI MS 13,504)

Gladstone Intervenes

On 25 November 1890 the Irish Parliamentary Party held a routine eve-of-session meeting in Committee Room Fifteen at the House of Commons to elect a chairman. The chairman was in effect the leader of the party, and Parnell had held the position since 1880. Before the meeting Gladstone informed Justin McCarthy that his supporters no longer wished him to associate with Parnell. He claimed that if Parnell continued as chairman of the Irish party the Liberals would lose the next general election and Home Rule would not be possible for the foreseeable future.

Although McCarthy told Parnell of Gladstone's intervention, the meeting was not informed and Parnell was unanimously re-elected chairman. When Gladstone heard this he immediately published a letter outlining his position which he had sent the previous day to his colleague John Morley.

Mr Gladstone and Mr Parnell

The following letter from Mr Gladstone to Mr John Morley was communicated to Mr Parnell in the course of yesterday afternoon:–

1 Carlton Gardens, November 24, 1890.

My Dear Morley, – Having arrived at a certain conclusion with regard to the continuance at the present moment of Mr Parnell's leadership of the Irish party, I have seen Mr McCarthy on my arrival in town, and have inquired from him whether I was likely to receive from Mr Parnell himself any communication on the subject. Mr McCarthy replied that he was unable to give me any communication on the subject. I mentioned to him that in 1882, after the terrible murder in the Phoenix Park, Mr Parnell, although totally removed from any idea of responsibility, had spontaneously written to me and offered to take the Chiltern Hundreds [i.e.resign from parliament], an offer much to his honour, but one which I thought it my duty to decline.

While clinging to the hope of a communication from Mr Parnell to whomsoever addressed, I thought it necessary, viewing the arrangements for the commencement of the session tomorrow, to acquaint Mr McCarthy with the conclusion at which, after using all the means of observation and reflection in my power, I had myself arrived. It was that, notwithstanding the splendid services rendered by Mr Parnell to his country, his continuance at the present moment in the leadership would be productive of consequences disastrous in the highest degree to the cause of Ireland. I think I may be warranted in asking you so far to explain the conclusion I have given above as to add that the continuance which I speak of would not only place many hearty and effective friends of the Irish cause in a position of great embarrassment, but would render my retention of the leadership of the Liberal party, based as it has been mainly upon the prosecution of the Irish cause, almost a nullity. ...

I now write to you in case Mr McCarthy should be unable to communicate with Mr Parnell, as I understand you may possibly have an opening tomorrow through another channel. Should you have such an opening I would beg you to make known to Mr Parnell the conclusion itself, which I have stated in the earlier part of this letter. I have thought it best to put it in terms simple and direct, much as I should have desired had it been within my power to alleviate the painful nature of the situation. As respects the manner of conveying what my public duty has made it an obligation to say, I rely entirely on your good feeling, tact, and judgement.

Believe me, sincerely yours,
W.E. Gladstone.
To Right Hon. John Morley, MP.

(Pall Mall Gazette, 26 November 1890)

The re-election of Parnell as chairman of the Irish Parliamentary Party. At the table to Parnell's right are, Justin McCarthy, Richard Power (standing), Thomas Sexton (standing), J. O'Kelly, David Sheehy, Dr Tanner, J.Tuite, J.E. Redmond. On his left are Henry Campbell (his secretary), A. O'Connor, E. Harrington, Dr Kenny, Col. J.P. Nolan. *(Illustrated London News, 6 December 1890)*

The Manifesto and the Bishops

Parnell's response to Gladstone's announcement was to issue a manifesto which appeared in the newspapers on 29 November 1890. In it he revealed the gist of the confidential discussions which had taken place at Hawarden the previous December, and he claimed that Gladstone's proposals for Home Rule were unsatisfactory. He recommended that the Irish party should abandon the Liberal alliance and revert to its traditional policy of remaining independent of all British parties. As he had already publicly asserted his satisfaction with the Hawarden discussions, his attitude at this stage damaged his credibility. He afterwards admitted that the tactic of the manifesto was a mistake.

A meeting of the parliamentary party convened on 1 December in Committee Room Fifteen at the House of Commons to consider the situation. While the meeting of the parliamentary party continued, the Standing Committee of the Irish bishops met on 3 December and issued a statement.

To the People of Ireland

The integrity and independence of a section of the Irish Parliamentary Party having been sapped and destroyed by the wire-pullers of the English Liberal Party, it has become necessary for me as the Leader of the Irish Nation to take counsel with you and, having given you the knowledge which is within my possession, to ask your judgement upon a matter which now solely devolves upon you to decide.

The letter of Mr Gladstone to Mr Morley, written for the purpose of influencing the decision of the Irish Party in the choice of their leader, and claiming for the Liberal Party and their leaders the right of veto upon that choice, is the immediate cause of this address to you, to remind you and your parliamentary representatives that Ireland considers the independence of her Party as her only safeguard within the Constitution and above and beyond all other considerations whatever. The threat in that letter, repeated so insolently on many English platforms and in numerous British newspapers, that unless Ireland concedes this right of veto to England she will indefinitely postpone her chances of obtaining Home Rule, compels me, while not for one moment admitting the slightest probability of such loss, to put before you information which until now, so far as my colleagues are concerned, has been solely in my possession, and which will enable you to understand the measure of the loss with which you are threatened unless you consent to throw me to the English wolves now howling for my destruction.

In November of last year, in response to a repeated and long-standing request, I visited Mr Gladstone at Hawarden, and received the details of the intended proposal of himself and his colleagues of the late Liberal Cabinet with regard to Home Rule, in the event of the next general election favouring the Liberal Party.

It is unnecessary for me to do more at present than to direct your attention to certain points of these details, which will be generally recognised as embracing elements vital for your information and the formation of your judgement. These vital points of difficulty may be suitably arranged and considered under the following heads: ...

Extract from a draft of Parnell's manifesto. On 22 July 1921 the former Parnellite MP, Dr J.G. Fitzgerald, sent it to Arthur Griffith for presentation to President De Valera. (NLI MS 21,933)

Sixteen years ago I conceived the idea of an Irish Parliamentary Party independent of all English parties. Ten years ago I was elected the leader of an independent Irish Parliamentary Party. During these ten years that Party has remained independent, and because of its independence it has forced upon the English people the necessity of granting Home Rule to Ireland. I believe that Party will obtain Home Rule only provided it remains independent of any English party.

I do not believe that any action of the Irish people in supporting me will endanger the Home Rule cause or postpone the establishment of an Irish Parliament; but even if the danger with which we are threatened by the Liberal Party of to-day were to be realised, I believe that the Irish people throughout the world would agree with me that postponement would be preferable to a compromise of our national rights by the acceptance of a measure which would not realise the aspirations of our race.

I have the honour to remain, Your faithful servant, CHARLES STEWART PARNELL.

(*Freeman's Journal*, 29 November 1890)

Address of the Standing Committee of the Archbishops and Bishops of Ireland to the Clergy and Laity of their Flocks:–

Very Reverend and Reverend Fathers and fellow-countrymen – The Bishops of Ireland can no longer keep silent in presence of the all-engrossing question which agitates, not Ireland and England alone, but every spot where Irishmen have found a home. That question is – Who is to be in future the Leader of the Irish people or, rather, Who is not to be their Leader.

Without hesitation or doubt, and in the plainest possible terms, we give it as our unanimous judgement that, whoever else is fit to fill that highly responsible post, Mr Parnell decidedly is not.

As Pastors of this Catholic nation, we do not base this, our judgement and solemn declaration, on political grounds, but simply and solely on the facts and circumstances revealed in the London Divorce Court.

After the verdict given in that Court, we cannot regard Mr Parnell in any other light than as a man convicted of one of the gravest offences known to religion and society, aggravated as it is in this case by almost every circumstance that could possibly attach to it so as to give it a scandalous pre-eminence in guilt and shame. Surely, Catholic Ireland, so eminently conspicuous for its virtue and the purity of its social life, will not accept as its leader a man thus dishonoured and wholly unworthy of Christian confidence.

Furthermore, as Irishmen devoted to our country, eager for its elevation and earnestly intent on securing for it the benefits of domestic legislation, we cannot but be influenced by the conviction that the continuance of Mr Parnell as leader of even a section of the Irish party must have the effect of disorganising our ranks, and ranging as in hostile camps the hitherto united forces of our country.

Confronted with the prospect of contingencies so disastrous, we see nothing but inevitable defeat at the approaching general election and, as a result, Home Rule indefinitely postponed, coercion perpetuated, the hands of the Evictor strengthened, and the tenants already evicted left without the shadow of a hope of being ever restored to their homes.

Your devoted servants in Christ,

Michael Logue, Archbishop of Armagh, Primate of All Ireland
William J. Walsh, Archbishop of Dublin, Primate of Ireland
T.W. Croke, Archbishop of Cashel
John McEvilly, Archbishop of Tuam
Laurence Gillooly, Bishop of Elphin
James Donnelly, Bishop of Clogher
James Lynch, Bishop of Kildare and Leighlin
Francis J. MacCormac, Bishop of Galway and Kilmacduagh
John MacCarthy, Bishop of Cloyne
William Fitzgerald, Bishop of Ross
Bartholomew Woodlock, Bishop of Ardagh and Clonmacnoise
Thomas Alphonsus O'Callaghan, Bishop of Cork
James Browne, Bishop of Ferns
Abraham Brownrigg, Bishop of Ossory
Patrick MacAlister, Bishop of Down and Connor
Patrick O'Donnell, Bishop of Raphoe
John Lyster, Bishop of Achonry
Edward Magennis, Bishop of Kilmore
Thomas McGivern, Bishop of Dromore
John K. O'Doherty, Bishop of Derry
Michael Comerford, Co-adjutor Bishop of Kildare and Leighlin
Thos McRedmond, Co-adjutor Bishop of Killaloe
Nicholas Donnelly, Bishop of Canea (Auxiliary Bishop of Dublin)

(*Freeman's Journal*, 4 December 1890)

Committee Room Fifteen

The discussions in Committee Room Fifteen dragged on until 6 December. From an early stage it was apparent that the majority now believed that Parnell should resign. However, Parnell skilfully diverted the discussion to a consideration of Gladstone's plans for Home Rule. He claimed that he was willing to retire if Gladstone gave satisfactory assurances regarding the provisions of a future Home Rule bill. A delegation met Gladstone but he was unwilling to give specific commitments at that stage.

At the party meeting tempers became frayed, and Parnell snatched and crumpled William Abraham's proposal that his tenure of the chairmanship be terminated. As there seemed no prospect of a satisfactory outcome, the forty-five MPs who opposed Parnell withdrew on the evening of 6 December. They held a meeting in another room and passed a resolution terminating Parnell's chairmanship. They then elected Justin McCarthy chairman. However, Parnell and the MPs who remained with him claimed that that action was invalid and that Parnell was still chairman of the party. A number of MPs were not present at the meetings in Committee Room Fifteen; most of them subsequently declared against Parnell.

House of Commons, 6th December, 1890.

We are within a few minutes of disruption. We cannot get the Liberals to say anything while Parnell remains chairman, and he refuses to allow any resolution to be moved requiring him to resign. We had a row to-day as he called upon John O'Connor to move a resolution, when we wished William Abraham to be heard. We shouted for him, and there was slight disorder. Abraham handed his resolution to McCarthy, and we called on McCarthy to put it. Parnell roared that he would not allow him to act as chairman, and snatched the paper out of his hand. McCarthy did not know what was in the paper. Sexton appealed to the meeting to hear O'Connor for a short time, as we did not intend to remain listening to obstructive speeches. McCarthy rose and dignifiedly explained that he had risen to a point of order when Parnell snapped a paper out of his hand. Parnell made a kind of apology, and O'Connor was heard to move a resolution against Gladstone.

In the midst of his speech John Redmond shouted that Gladstone would be 'master of the party'. I asked, 'who would be the mistress of the party?' Whereupon Parnell called me 'a dirty little scoundrel who insulted a woman'. I made no reply, being content with the thrust which will stick as long as his cry about Gladstone's 'dictation' continues. I knew compromise would be impossible. ...

– Letter of Tim Healy to his wife.

(T.M. Healy, *Letters*, ii, 336)

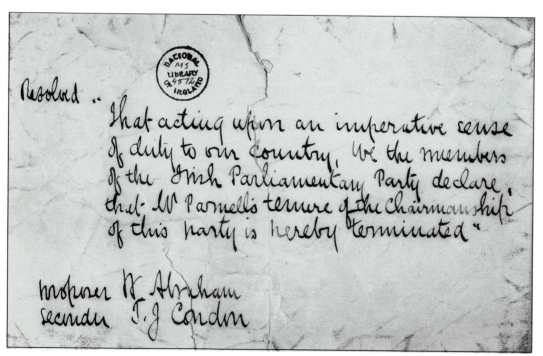

William Abraham's resolution. The document was taken away by Justin McCarthy who gave it to Ms Elspeth Grahame. She deposited it in the National Library of Ireland. (NLI MS 4572)

Mr Justin McCarthy Asks the Majority to Leave

... Mr Justin McCarthy – Mr Chairman and gentlemen, I think the time has quite come when we ought to bring the debate to a close ('hear, hear'). I think there is no possibility whatever now of our being allowed to bring this question to a test. I do not want to add one single word to increase the bitterness of a crisis like this. I had hoped up to last night that our Chairman would still help us out of this terrible, this national, this organic difficulty and crisis. I may say to him that I am personally disappointed that he has not lent us more assistance out of this terrible dilemma into which we have been brought, but I feel that we did waste our time, and the time of our opponents, in further controversy where it has been made clear that the door is to be barred against any definite settlement of the controversy in this room within any reasonable limit ('hear, hear', and 'no, no').

I therefore feel that the longer we debate, the more we may possibly grow in passion, the more we may become unkindly, the more bitter things we may say, and I may add that if bitter things have been said from my side, I for my own part, and I am sure all my friends join with me, we deeply regret it ('hear, hear'). I see no further use carrying on a discussion which must be barren of all but reproach, ill-temper, controversy, and indignity, and I will therefore suggest that all who think with me at this grave crisis should withdraw with me from this room (loud cheers).

The majority then left the room, leaving Mr Parnell in the chair and the following members – Messrs Leamy, J. Redmond, W. Redmond, J.J. O'Kelly, G.M. Byrne, A. Blane, W.J. Corbet, Joseph Nolan, R. Maguire, H. Harrison, J. Dalton, W.A. MacDonald, M. Conway, T. Quinn, J.J. Clancy, Pierce Mahony, J.P. Hayden, Colonel Nolan, Dr Fitzgerald, E. Harrington, R. Power, E. Shiel, H. Campbell, J. O'Connor, Dr Kenny, and Sir J. McKenna. ...

(*Freeman's Journal*, 8 December 1890)

THE MEETING OF THE MAJORITY
Important Resolution
(From our Reporters)
London, Sunday.

The forty-five members of the Irish party who left the meeting in Committee Room Fifteen immediately adjourned to the Conference Room of the House of Commons, and held a meeting for the purpose of passing resolutions declaring Mr Parnell's leadership terminated and electing a successor. ...

On the proposition of Mr Abraham, seconded by Mr D. Sheehy, the following declaration was agreed to:–

We hereby solemnly renew our adhesion to the principle in devotion to which we have never wavered – viz, that the Irish Parliamentary Party is, and always must remain, independent of all other parties; and we further declare that we will never entertain any proposal for the settlement of the Home Rule question except such as satisfies the aspirations of the Irish people.

Signed:

Justin McCarthy, Derry City, Chairman; William Abraham, West Limerick; J. Barry, South Wexford; P.A. Chance, South Kilkenny; A. Commins, South Roscommon; T.F. Condon, Tipperary; J.A. Cox, East Clare; Daniel Crilly, North Mayo; J. Deasy, Cork; T.A. Dickson, Stephen's Green, Dublin; T.H. Grattan Esmonde, South Co. Dublin; John Finucane, East Limerick; J.C. Flynn, North Cork; P.J. Foley, Connemara; J.F. Fox, King's County; M. Healy, Cork; T.M. Healy, North Longford; J. Jordan, West Clare; M.J. Kenny, Mid Tyrone; Denis Kilbride, South Kerry; E.F. Knox, West Cavan; W.J. Lane, East Cork; M. McCartan, South Down; Justin H. McCarthy, Newry; P. McDonald, North Sligo; P.G. Swift McNeill, South Donegal; Bernard C. Molloy, Birr Division, King's County; P. Morrough, South East Cork; W. Murphy, St Patrick's Division, Dublin; J.F.X. O'Brien, South Mayo; P.J. O'Brien, North Tipperary; A. O'Connor, East Donegal; F.A. O'Keeffe, Limerick City; J. Pinkerton, Galway City; P.J. Power, East Waterford; W.J. Reynolds, East Tyrone; John Roche, East Galway; T. Sexton, West Belfast; P.D. Sheehan, East Kerry; D. Sheehy, South Galway; J. Stack, North Kerry; D. Sullivan, South Westmeath; C.R. Tanner, Mid Cork; J. Tuite, North Westmeath; A. Webb, West Waterford.

(*Freeman's Journal*, 8 December 1890)

'The Crow-bar King'

The editor of United Ireland, *William O'Brien, who was in the United States, instructed his deputy, Matthew Bodkin, to reflect the views of the majority of the Irish Parliamentary Party on the leadership issue. Accordingly, the issue of 6 December was hostile to Parnell. Four days later Parnell arrived in Dublin and dismissed Bodkin. Later the anti-Parnellites re-occupied the office of* United Ireland *in Lower Abbey Street, whereupon Parnell and his supporters rushed to the scene. An eye-witness gave a graphic account of Parnell as the man of action.* St. Stephen's Review, *a hostile magazine, afterwards dubbed Parnell, 'The Crow-bar King'.*

Seizure of *United Ireland*

There was a brief discussion. Then Parnell suddenly realised that the fort might be carried from the area door. In a moment he was on the point of vaulting the railings. The hands of considerate friends restrained him by force. I heard his voice ring out clearly, impatiently, imperatively: 'Go yourselves, if you will not let me.' At the word several of those around him dropped into the area. Now Parnell snatched the crowbar and, swinging his arms with might and main, thundered at the door. The door yielded and, followed by those nearest to him, he disappeared into the hall. Instantly up rose a terrible noise. The other storming party, it seems, had entered from the area and, rushing upstairs, had crashed into Parnell's bodyguard. What happened within the house I do not know for spectators outside could only hold their breath and listen and guess. Feet clattered on the boarded stairs, voices hoarse with rage shrieked and shouted. A veritable pandemonium was let loose. At last there was a lull within, broken by the cheers of the waiting crowd without. One of the windows on the second storey was removed, and Parnell suddenly appeared in the aperture. He had conquered. The enthusiasm which greeted him cannot be described. His face was ghastly pale, save only that on either cheek a hectic crimson spot was glowing. His hat was off now, his hair dishevelled, the dust of the conflict begrimed his well-brushed coat. The people were spell-bound, almost terrified, as they gazed on him. For myself, I felt a thrill of dread, as if I looked at a tiger in a frenzy of its rage. Then he spoke, and the tone of his voice was even more terrible than his look. He was brief, rapid, decisive, and the closing words of his speech still ring in my ear: 'I rely on Dublin. Dublin is true. What Dublin says today Ireland will say to-morrow'.

(R.B. O'Brien, *Life of Parnell*, ii, 295-6)

Supplement Gratis with "UNITED IRELAND." Saturday. December 6th. 1890.

FOR IRELAND AND LIBERTY

FOR PARNELL

DISSENSION

UNDER WHICH FLAG?

CHAPTER IX

The Last Campaign

At the split almost two thirds of the parliamentary party, including most of the more prominent and able members, defected from Parnell. Before the end of 1890 the North Kilkenny by-election provided a test of the strength of the two sides in the country. The result indicated that Parnell had the support of less than one third of the electorate. In the circumstances it is surprising that he did not grasp the opportunity for an honourable settlement presented shortly after at the Boulogne negotiations. The terms proposed at Boulogne would have enabled him to retire from the chairmanship with dignity and at the same time retain most of his power and influence until he could again resume his position as the formal leader of the party.

However, by that stage the argument had become so personalised and bitter that he was probably not disposed to entertain any compromise, no matter how favourable. He had been labouring under intense mental and physical strain for a considerable period, and he may not have been as detached and realistic in his judgement as the situation warranted. Moreover, his style had always been that of the man of action and his instinct was to take the offensive. Many times before he had faced up to formidable odds, and no doubt he believed that on this occasion also there was a worthwhile chance that he would eventually prevail.

Events were to prove that he was mistaken, and as the year 1891 wore on his fortunes were obviously in decline. In March his opponents established a new organisation, the Irish National Federation, in opposition to the Irish National League which remained under his control. They also set up their own newspaper, the *National Press,* which produced a stream of damaging and personalised invective. Parnell appealed to the Irish in the United States for funds to promote his campaign but, on this occasion, with little success. By-elections were held in North Sligo and Carlow in April and July, and on both occasions his candidates were defeated.

In this scenario which was becoming increasingly depressing for Parnell, the one bright spot was his marriage to Katharine O'Shea on 25 June. Now that their relationship was regularised, it might have been expected that the hostility on the moral issue would be defused. On the contrary, some people regarded the marriage as compounding the original offence of adultery, and the hostility escalated rather than diminished. The marriage had an especially serious consequence in that it prompted the *Freeman's Journal* to transfer its allegiance to the opposition. Parnell's reaction was typical and he proceeded at once to set up a morning and an evening newspaper over which he would have complete control. The title of the morning paper, the *Irish Daily Independent,* was intended to reflect his attitude to the alliance with the Liberals which was central to the split. However, as it turned out he was already dead for some months when the newspapers appeared.

The Kilkenny Election

A by-election was scheduled to take place in North Kilkenny on 22 December, and it provided a trial of strength for the two sides. The original party candidate, Sir John Pope-Hennessy, declared for the anti-Parnellites, and Parnell then nominated Vincent Scully. The atmosphere of the election campaign was tense and bitter, and on a number of occasions the supporters of both parties behaved disgracefully. After a meeting at Castlecomer, lime was thrown at Parnell and his eye was injured. The result of the election was that Parnell's candidate was defeated by a majority of almost two to one. This was a fair indication of the strength of the two parties in the country at large.

December 10, 1890.

My Dear Lord,

I feel sure your Grace would like to know from some authentic source how matters stand on the first battle-ground of the present crisis.

There is thorough unanimity between myself and all sections of the priests. Yesterday the priests of the city have met and passed unanimously the resolutions which appear in the papers today. On tomorrow the priests of the three deaneries of the diocese are to meet, and I have no reason to think that the slightest diversity of opinion will prevail. Happily in every single instance, but one, in the diocese the local branches of the League are presided over by the priests, so that we may regard them as reflecting the views of the clergy. Last Sunday I find there were meetings of the several branches thro' the diocese, and in every single instance but one (and that the one in which the priests have nothing to do) the opinion was entirely against Parnell.

If this weight of opinion can be maintained thro' the agitation which will precede the election, there can be no doubt of Pope-Hennessy's return. This is certain that there is not a spot in all Ireland where a battle could be fought more favourably for us and as against Parnell than in North Kilkenny. However, we must be wary, our enemies are very cunning and our poor people are very easily influenced. Unfortunately, too, there are short turns in the Irish character, and voting by ballot affords an opportunity, which is sometimes availed of, of betraying public faith. It is well for us that Parnell's career has come to an end, for we now see how infatuated our people are about him even in his disgrace and when he has brought such ruin on our country. Your Grace can rely on us here to do all that is possible on the right side.

I am, your Grace, Most devotedly yours in Christ, A. Brownrigg.

– Letter of Dr Abraham Brownrigg, Bishop of Ossory, to Dr Walsh, Archbishop of Dublin.

(Dublin Diocesan Archives, Archbishop Walsh Papers)

Meeting at Castlecomer

When Mr Parnell sat down, the brake was driven up the street of the town, and the moment it began to move there came a shower of slaked lime and mud which was continued until all the occupants of the brake were covered. Mr Parnell was struck in the eyes with a bag of this lime, and one of his eyes was somewhat injured.

... Meanwhile the Irish leader was sitting in front of the fire with a white handkerchief tied over his right eye. When he came to the window he received a great cheer, and the speech which he made was full of fire. He has seldom appeared more dramatic and striking, and about all the sentences there was that ring of earnestness which showed confidence in his strength and power. He never appeared more resolute or determined, and the effect upon his hearers, standing together in the darkness of the night and with uplifted faces, was electric. The incident of this speech had about it a great deal that was pathetic as well as soul-stirring, and there were none present who will forget this strongly-touching scene.

(*Freeman's Journal*, 17 December 1890

Mr Parnell's Speech

Immediately after the declaration of the poll and the passing of the usual vote of thanks, a scene of great excitement took place outside the courthouse. The street in front was quite blocked with people, while an enormous force of police was present. The news of the result was quickly disseminated through the people, who at once gave token of their dissatisfaction by vigorous groaning.

As Sir John Pope-Hennessy's supporters came out on the balcony of the courthouse, they were hooted and howled at by the immense crowd. Mr Michael Davitt appeared on the balcony in company with several priests, and his appearance was the sign for renewed groaning and booing, while the priests and a few people in the crowd cheered. Mr Davitt had hardly left the balcony when Mr Parnell appeared. At once he was surrounded and chaired by a cheering and enthusiastic crowd. When he was able to make his way to the front of the balcony the immense crowd on the street cheered wildly, and Mr Parnell could not for some minutes gain a hearing.

When silence had been restored, Mr Parnell said – Men of Kilkenny, although we have been defeated (cries of 'never' and cheers) – in this one single battle out of the eighty-six which are before us, we are undaunted (prolonged cheering), and we promise you that we will rise through this defeat to ultimate and universal victory (loud cheers).

(*Freeman's Journal*, 24-25 December 1890)

Parnell making a speech some days after the Castlecomer incident. (*Illustrated London News*, 27 December 1890)

The Boulogne Negotiations

At the time of the leadership crisis, William O'Brien, John Dillon and T.P. Gill were on a fund-raising mission in the United States. After the split on 6 December they made a final effort to resolve the dispute. O'Brien and Dillon were liable to imprisonment if they landed in Ireland or Britain, and the three arranged to meet Parnell and his representatives at Boulogne. The negotiations took place between 30 December 1890 and 11 February 1891.

The formula proposed would enable Parnell to retain the substance of his power. However, it was too optimistic in that it expected the Liberals and the bishops to withdraw from their positions. As in Committee Room Fifteen, Parnell again tried to get guarantees from the Liberals as to the content of a future Home Rule bill. When the guarantees failed to satisfy him, the attempt at a resolution was abandoned.

Terms Proposed by William O'Brien at Boulogne

1. Meeting of the whole party; acknowledgement of informality of McCarthy's election, and re-election of McCarthy as chairman by agreement of whole party.

2. All possible personal satisfaction in shape of public declaration of party expressing gratitude, and enumerating circumstances of misunderstanding tending to account for conflict.

3. All possible efforts to be made to secure from Gladstone acknowledgement of mistake of precipitate publication of his letter, and admission that he had not taken sufficient account of national sentiment in Ireland and of Parnell's position.

4. Possible retraction, in some shape, of bishops' manifesto by Dr Croke or Dr Walsh.

5. Vote of party only to affect chairmanship of party; P. to continue president of the National League; and, if desirable, prominent men of both sections to accompany him to a meeting, under his presidency, of the central branch in Dublin.

6. In case committee appointed by party, Parnell to have nomination of half thereof.

7. Any special recognition of Parnell that he can suggest that would secure his influence in all negotiations touching the Home Rule bill or other Irish legislation.

8. In case of agreement on these lines, O'Brien to decline chairmanship of new newspaper company [*The National Press*], and any rival committee to National League to be discouraged.

(*Freeman's Journal*, 12 November 1891)

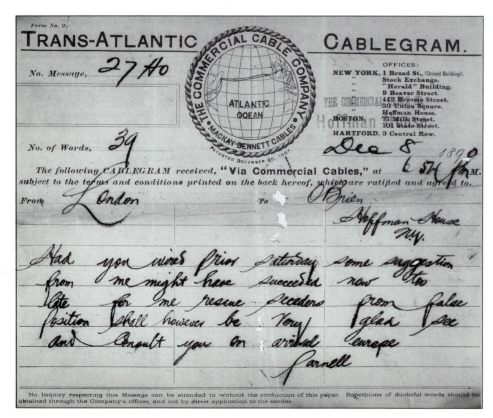

Telegram from Parnell to William O'Brien agreeing to meet him on his return from the United States. (NLI MS 13,506)

THE BOULOGNE CONFERENCE.

TERMINATION OF THE PROCEEDINGS.

A PEACEFUL SETTLEMENT EXPECTED.

INTERVIEW WITH MR. WM. O'BRIEN.

(FROM OUR SPECIAL REPRESENTATIVE.)
Boulogne, Wednesday.

The conference between the Irish members here terminated to day, having lasted all the morning until the departure of the boat for Folkestone. By this boat Mr. Parnell, M P; Mr. T Harrington, M P; Mr. J J Clancy, M P; Mr. Henry Campbell, M P; Mr. Vincent Scully, and Mr. Edward Byrne left on their way to London. Mr. William O'Brien, M P, and Mr. T P Gill, M P, remain until to-morrow, when they will return to Paris. Mr. John O'Connor, M P, will return to London to-morrow.

(Freeman's Journal, 8 January 1891)

William O'Brien (1850-1928). He made strenuous efforts to arrange a settlement but finally declared against Parnell in July. (NLI P&D)

To William O'Brien, MP,

February 11, 1891.

My Dear O'Brien,

The last information which Gill has conveyed to me on the subject of our negotiations being of a final character, I conclude there is nothing left to be done so far as I am concerned but to bring these endeavours of ours to arrive at a peaceful settlement of the unhappy differences in our party to a close. I regret that it has not been rendered possible for me to consider the national interest so safeguarded, that I could feel there would be no danger to the cause in my now surrendering the responsibility which has been placed upon me, and which I have accepted at the hands of our nation and our race. I had been ready to act up to the letter and the spirit of our understanding to the last moment, and I regret then there is no course left to me now but to withdraw from the negotiations. ...

In any event and on whichever side true Irishmen may be engaged in this controversy, they owe you thanks for the beneficient efforts you have made, and I am sure the country will agree that you have acted throughout in the spirit of a true patriot.

Believe me,
My Dear O'Brien,
Yours Very Sincerely,

Charles Stewart Parnell.

– Transcript of Parnell's letter to O'Brien in the T.P. Gill Papers.

(NLI MS 13,507)

Marriage

Parnell and Katharine O'Shea were eventually married in a registry office at Steyning near Brighton on 25 June 1891. At the time they were living at Walsingham Terrace, Brighton.

Parnell sent the news by telegram to J.M. Tuohy at the London office of the Freeman's Journal. The verso of one of the sheets has a note in Tuohy's hand: 'The first document in which he has ever put his private address', a reference to the fact that for ten years Parnell tried to hide the fact that he was living with Mrs O'Shea.

The telegram announcing the marriage. (NLI MS 5934)

Marriage

On June 25th I was awakened at daybreak by my lover's tapping at my door and calling to me: 'Get up, get up, it is time to be married!' Then a humming and excitement began through the house as the maids flew about to get us and breakfast ready 'in time', before two of them, Phyllis Bryson, my very dear personal maid – who had put off her own marriage for many years in order to remain with me – and my children's old nurse, drove off to catch the early train to Steyning, where they were to be witnesses of our marriage. Phyllis was so determined to put the finishing touches to me herself that she was at last hustled off by Parnell, who was in a nervous fear that everyone would be late but the newspaper men. Phyllis was fastening a posy at my breast when Parnell gently but firmly took it from her and replaced it with white roses he had got for me the day before. Seeing her look of disappointment he said, 'She must wear mine today, Phyllis, but she shall carry yours, and you shall keep them in remembrance; now you must go!'

As a rule Parnell never noticed what I wore. Clothes were always 'things' to him. 'Your things become you always', was the utmost compliment for a new gown I could ever extract from him; but that morning, as he climbed in beside me and I took the reins, he said, 'Queenie, you look lovely in that lace stuff and the beautiful hat with the roses! I am so proud of you!'

And I was proud of my King, of my wonderful lover, as we drove through that glorious June morning, past the fields of growing corn, by the hedges heavy with wild roses and 'traveller's joy,' round the bend of the river at Lancing, past the ruined tower where we had so often watched the kestrels hover, over the bridge and up the street of pretty, old-world Bramber into Steyning, and on to the consummation of our happiness.

Mr Cripps was in attendance, and Mrs Cripps had very charmingly decorated the little room with flowers, so there was none of the dreariness usual with a registry marriage. As we waited for our witnesses to arrive – we had beaten the train! – my King looked at us both in the small mirror on the wall of the little room and, adjusting his white rose in his frock-coat, said joyously: 'It isn't every woman who makes so good a marriage as you are making, Queenie, is it? and to such a handsome fellow, too!' blowing kisses to me in the glass. Then the two maids arrived, and the little ceremony that was to legalise our union of many years was quickly over.

On the return drive my husband pulled up the hood of the phaeton and to my questioning look – for it was a hot morning – he answered solemnly, 'it's the right thing to do.' As we drove off, bowing and laughing our thanks to Mr Cripps and the others for their kind and enthusiastic felicitations, he said: 'How could I kiss you good wishes for our married life unless we were hooded up like this!'

(K. O'Shea, *C.S.Parnell*, ii, 251-3)

The registrar's house at Steyning, Sussex, where the marriage took place. (*Daily Graphic*, 29 June 1891)

The Newspaper War

To carry on their campaigns both of the rival parties required money. Parnell seemed to have more than his opponents, and that led Archbishop Croke to enquire about various funds for which he had never provided proper accounts. These included the 'Parnell Tribute' of 1883, the Defence Fund raised at the time of the Special Commission, and a sum of £10,000 donated by Cecil Rhodes to promote Home Rule. In a speech at Wicklow Parnell made a rather inadequate reply to the query, and the following day Tim Healy issued the notorious 'Stop, Thief' article. However, John Dillon intervened and that line of attack was discontinued.

Parnell's marriage to Katharine O'Shea further offended the Catholic clergy and a bishop denounced it as 'the climax of brazened horrors'. Up to that stage, the Freeman's Journal *had supported Parnell, but the clerical denunciation of the marriage, and the repudiation of Parnell by John Dillon and William O'Brien on their release from prison, induced the principal shareholder, Edmund Dwyer Gray, to withdraw the paper's support.*

In August Parnell set about filling the gap created by the defection of the Freeman's Journal. *It was decided to publish a morning and an evening newspaper, 'to advocate the principles of Home Rule for Ireland and independent action in the House of Commons'. The* Irish Independent *Printing and Publishing Company was established soon after. However, the first issues of the* Irish Daily Independent *and the* Evening Herald *did not appear until 18 and 19 December 1891 when Parnell was already dead.*

Stop, Thief!

On his native heath at Wicklow yesterday Mr Parnell shirked in the most cowardly and hang-dog fashion the terrible indictment of Archbishop Croke. The speech at Kilteely was so scathing and irrefutable that it was suppressed on Saturday by the *Freeman's Journal,* which did not dare to let it go before the world until the careful and impartial press-men who manage the 'Chief's' kept organ, could ascertain from the Oracle how the burning and branding words of His Grace were to be treated. A paragraph was manufactured, however, in its London correspondence, stating that the deposed man would reply at Wicklow to 'both archbishops.' We give elsewhere the alleged 'reply'. As to the damning discourtesy with which the burrowing adulterer treated the Metropolitan of Munster no answer is attempted. On three separate days Mr Parnell made three different appointments in London to meet Dr Croke, and three times, with every addendum of scurvy insult, he disappointed the stranger at his gates. The archbishop did not seek the Elthamite to hobnob with him, to flatter him, to bask in his smiles, or beg of his favours. His mission was business. Mr Parnell could not have regarded it as stern, though it related to financial details, for all that was proposed was to suggest that the public conscience would be easier and the public generosity greater if a public audit into Parnellite accounts were made possible. This was in 1889, after the Commission had terminated satisfactorily – barring Mr Parnell's oath that he had deliberately lied to deceive the House of Commons, and, therefore the intervention of a notoriously friendly prelate could not have been mis-appreciated or denied on the score of hostility or intended eavesdropping. The silence of Mr Parnell now is the best explanation of his refusal to face, even in five minutes' friendly conversation, a powerful and determined Nationalist. Why? Because for years he has been stealing the money entrusted to his charge.

(*National Press,* 1 June 1891)

Pembroke House, Upper Mount Street, Dublin.

July 31.

To the editor of the *Freeman*

Dear Sir - Now that Mr William O'Brien and Mr John Dillon have definitely declared themselves against the leadership of Mr Parnell, I can no longer, in justice to myself, withhold the fact that for some time past my views have been almost exactly similar to those expressed with such lucidity and force by Mr John Dillon yesterday.

Mr Parnell, by his recent marriage, has rendered it impossible that he should ever be recognised by the Catholic Hierarchy as the leader of a Catholic people of Ireland. Mr Parnell has thus by his own act, and with full knowledge of the consequences, rendered himself absolutely impossible as the leader of a united people. The marriage is no marriage according to the teaching of the Catholic Church, and it is simply preposterous to think of carrying on the national movement under a leader to whom the Church is unanimously opposed. ...

These things, taken in connection with the fact that three Irish counties have declared against Mr Parnell, seem to me to leave me no alternative but to advocate a change of leadership.

I supported Mr Parnell until he himself made it impossible for me to do so by removing by his own act, the doubt as to certain occurrences which I, among many others, shared up to a very recent date.

As the owner of nearly half the property of the *Freeman's Journal,* I might be held responsible. Under these circumstances I desire to make it perfectly clear at once that I am at one with Mr J. Dillon and Mr O'Brien.

I am, dear sir,
Yours truly,
E. Dwyer Gray.

(*Freeman's Journal,* 31 July 1891)

The proposal to establish an independent newspaper.
(NLI MS 10,514)

The Campaign Trail

Right to the end, Parnell kept up a relentless campaign around the country. He vigorously attacked the other side on all possible issues, and claimed that only his policy of independence from the British parties could ensure that a satisfactory measure of Home Rule was achieved. He looked for support from whoever might be prepared to give it, and in this period he courted such diverse interests as the industrial workers, the Ulster unionists and the small farmers of the West. In his increasingly difficult situation, he did at least succeed in again attracting the support of the Fenians to his cause. He also campaigned for the support of the Irish in Britain and addressed meetings at various centres but, as in Ireland, the response was mixed. He lost by-elections in North Sligo and Carlow, and by the autumn it was obvious to most observers that he was fighting a losing battle.

(*Daily Graphic*, 22 January 1891)

Some "Hill side" men. discussing Mr Parnell

Parnell addressing the London-Irish at Foresters' Hall, Clerkenwell. (*Daily Graphic*, 6 March 1891)

CHAPTER X

Death and Aftermath

In 1891 Parnell drove himself harder than ever before in his career. Almost every weekend he made the long and hacking journey by train and boat from Brighton to Dublin, and from there on to meetings and rallies around the country. At the same time the humiliation of his position, which was becoming increasingly hopeless, must have been hard to bear for a man of such a proud disposition. Eventually, the combination of physical hardship and mental stress undermined his health. In his latter years he may have had latent coronary artery disease, the pathology of which was not then fully understood. By the early autumn of 1891 it seems to have become acute, and it was aggravated by his final journey to Ireland when he addressed a meeting in the rain at Creggs, Co. Galway. After a few days illness he died at his home in Brighton on 6 October 1891, attended by his wife Katharine.

The people of Dublin had generally remained loyal to Parnell, and the funeral to Glasnevin was the greatest public occasion in the capital since the death of Daniel O'Connell in 1847. Many of the more fanatical of his followers found it difficult to come to terms with his death. Wild rumours persisted that he had been poisoned or that he had committed suicide, and indeed some claimed that he had not really died but was biding his time in some safe haven until the people realised their mistake and he could make a triumphal return to Irish politics.

If anything, Parnell's tragic death widened the rift between the rival parties and they were not re-united until 1900. John Redmond succeeded Parnell as leader, but in the general election of 1892, out of a total of eighty-one nationalist MPs, only nine Parnellites were returned. Regarding Parnell's ultimate objective, Home Rule, Gladstone succeeded in getting a bill through the House of Commons in 1893, but it was vetoed by the Lords. Home Rule was eventually enacted in 1914 but was suspended for the duration of World War I. However, in the aftermath of the 1916 Rising, Home Rule was no longer an adequate solution for the majority of nationalists, and the old Fenian ideal of complete independence became the objective. As in Parnell's time, the unionists opposed any form of Home Rule or independence and the country was partitioned in 1920-21.

Parnell had intended that Katharine should inherit Avondale but because of legal complications it went instead to his brother, John Howard. In any case, the estate was encumbered by debt and had to be sold in 1900. It was afterwards purchased by the Board of Agriculture for use as a forestry school. The house and demesne are now in the care of Coillte Teoranta and are open to the public at specified times.

Katharine remained a widow and mourned Parnell for almost thirty years until her death in 1921. Their two surviving daughters, Clare and Katharine, continued to be known as O'Sheas. Both married and had children but the line has long since died out.

Death

By the autumn of 1891 Parnell's health had deteriorated to an alarming degree. Nevertheless, he insisted on honouring all his engagements, and against the advice of his wife he travelled from their home in Brighton to address a meeting at Creggs, Co. Galway, on Sunday, 27 September. He got wet at the meeting and was feeling ill and feverish when he arrived home some days later. He was confined to bed for a few days and died on the night of 6 October 1891 at the age of forty-five. His life-long superstition that, for him, October was an unlucky month proved justified.

The symptoms of Parnell's final illness suggest that he was suffering from coronary heart disease. For some weeks he had a severe pain in the left arm. This is more likely to have been atypical angina pectoris than 'rheumatism' as was diagnosed at the time. His feeling towards the end that he was being held down by 'some strong unseen power' suggests that he was experiencing 'coronary insufficiency' preceding coronary thrombosis. Parnell was a heavy smoker and considering the level of stress to which he was subjected for many years, it is, perhaps, not surprising that he developed a heart condition. To some extent he may have inherited a tendency in this regard. His father also died suddenly, almost certainly of a heart attack, while still in his forties, and his sister Fanny died of a heart attack at the age of thirty-three.

Illness and Death

My husband was in great pain on the Monday, and seemed to feel a sudden horror that he was being held down by some strong unseen power, and asked my help – thank God, always my help – to fight against it. He tried to get out of bed, although he was too weak to stand, and I had to gently force him back and cover him up, telling him how dangerous a chill would be. He said: 'Hold me tight then, yourself, till I can fight those others.' Then he seemed to doze for a few minutes, and when he opened his eyes again it was to ask me to lie down beside him and put my hand in his, so that he could 'feel' I was there. I did so and he lay still, quite happy again, and spoke of the 'sunny land' where he would go as soon as he was better. 'We will be so happy, Queenie; there are so many things happier than politics.'

He did not sleep that night, and the next morning (Tuesday) he was very feverish, with a bright colour on his usually white face. I wanted to send the dogs from the room, because I feared they would disturb him, but he opened his eyes and said: 'Not Grouse; let old Grouse stay, I like him there.'

His doctor said that for a day or two we could not look for much improvement. After his medicine that afternoon he lay quietly with his eyes closed, just smiling if I touched him. The doctor came in again, but there was no change, and he left, promising to call early the next morning. During the evening my husband seemed to doze and, listening intently, I heard him mutter, 'the Conservative Party.'

Late in the evening he suddenly opened his eyes and said: 'Kiss me, sweet Wifie, and I will try to sleep a little.' I lay down by his side and kissed the burning lips he pressed to mine for the last time. The fire of them, fierce beyond any I had ever felt, even in his most loving moods, startled me, and as I slipped my hand from under his head he gave a little sigh and became unconscious. The doctor came at once, but no remedies prevailed against this sudden failure of the heart's action, and my husband died without regaining consciousness before his last kiss was cold on my lips.

There is little more to add. All that last night I sat by my husband watching and listening for the look and the word he would never give me again. All that night I whispered to him to speak to me, and I fancied that he moved, and that the fools who said he was dead did not really know. He had never failed to answer my every look and word before. His face was so peaceful; so well, all the tiredness had gone from it now. I would not open the door because I feared to disturb him – he had always liked us to be alone. And the rain and the wind swept about the house as though the whole world shared my desolation.

He did not make any 'dying speech', or refer in any way at the last to his 'Colleagues and the Irish people,' as was at the time erroneously reported. I was too broken then and too indifferent to what any sensation-lovers put about to contradict this story, but, as I am now giving to the world the absolutely true account of the Parnell whom I knew and loved, I am able to state that he was incapable of an affectation so complete. The last words Parnell spoke were given to the wife who had never failed him, to the love that was stronger than death – 'Kiss me, sweet Wifie, and I will try to sleep a little.'

(K. O'Shea, *C.S. Parnell*, ii, 274-6)

His Career

And who can speak of the private life of Mr Parnell? It is not – as one of the many writers on Mr Parnell once said – it is not easy to describe the mental life of a man who is neither expansive nor introspective: 'It is one of the strongest and most curious peculiarities of Mr Parnell, not merely that he rarely if ever speaks of himself, but that he rarely if ever gives any indication of having studied himself. His mind, if one may use the jargon of the Germans, is purely objective. There are few men who, after a certain length of acquaintance, do not familiarise you with the state of their hearts, or their stomachs, or their finances; with their fears, their hopes, their aims. But no man has ever been the confidant of Mr Parnell. Any allusion to himself by another, either in the exuberance of friendship or the design of flattery, is passed by unheeded, and it is a joke among his intimates that to Mr Parnell the being Parnell does not exist.' Whether the public will ever have the inner life of Mr Parnell opened to them it is idle now to speculate. It is enough to say it is not yet known. As for his public career, it is within the knowledge of even the youngest men. His political life is the history of this country for the past fifteen years. Less than a score of years ago he was a quiet young squire in his native Wicklow, scarcely known outside his own estate, some six and twenty years of age, a private gentleman, and much given to experiments in amateur engineering. Within the brief period that has since elapsed he has filled for a time the largest place in the political affairs of the kingdom. If he did not create a policy he at least adapted it with the greatest skill to the exigencies of his time. He became a leader of the Irish party and the Irish people with the powers of a dictator. He was a Warwick among Ministries. He was not ten years in parliament when the two great parties in the state were rivals for his favour. One party approached him surreptitiously through no less a personage than the Lord Lieutenant of Ireland. The other party, honestly believing that Mr Parnell was the mouthpiece of a nation, courageously accepted the situation and surrendered to his influence by adopting the principles he advocated.

(*Freeman's Journal*, 8 October 1891)

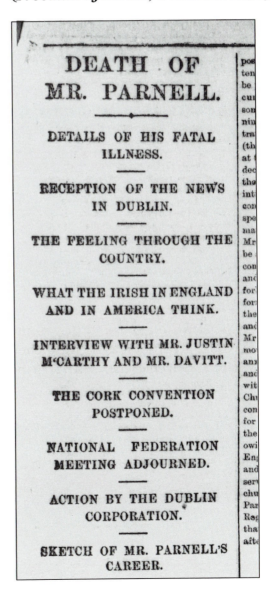

(*National Press*, 8 October 1891)

The Funeral

Following the announcement of Parnell's death a number of his followers went to Brighton, and it was arranged that the remains should be brought home to Ireland for a public funeral.

Mr Parnell's Funeral

The funeral of the late Irish leader has been an impressive and decorous ceremonial, with less of pomp than O'Connell's obsequies, but quite as national in its character, and heightened with a degree of gloom in harmony with the stern, 'dour' character of the dead man and the deep shadow in which his latter days were spent. The procession started from Walsingham Terrace, Brighton, on Saturday, October 10, the coffin of polished oak being borne on an open car drawn by four horses. A few wreaths were attached to the coffin, including one from his widow bearing the inscription, significant of the passionate attachment between her and Mr Parnell, 'To my true love, my husband.' At the railway station the most notable of Mr Parnell's adherents awaited the procession, and thence to the arrival at Dublin the body had a continuous escort of political and personal friends, Mrs Parnell remaining at Brighton. ...

The funeral leaving Parnell's house in Walsingham Terrace, Brighton. *(Illustrated London News,* 17 October 1891)

There was another solemn procession when the coffin, enclosed in a deal covering, was borne on the shoulders of the seamen to the boat at Holyhead, where another deputation from Dublin weepingly received it. At Kingstown Harbour the national part of the ceremonial began. Sunday morning dawned with chill grey skies and drenching rain, and it was dreary waiting for the *Ireland* with her sad burden. On the pier were waiting Parnellite members, municipal deputations, and members of Gaelic athletic societies, bearing their *cammáns* or clubs wreathed in black crepe, tied with a green ribbon. On the arrival at Dublin the crowd, for the first and only time, broke bounds, and a fierce struggle took place for the fragments of the deal covering of the coffin, which was hacked to pieces with knives and scrambled for with wild eagerness for preservation as relics. The Gaelic societies formed a guard of honour, the Irish colours were thrown over the hearse, and the mighty multitude, watched by a still vaster crowd, swept on from the Westland Row Station to the old church of St Michan, a dismal building of the twelfth century. Here the watchers within heard the melancholy tramp of the procession, and here the funeral service was read beginning with the words: 'I am the Resurrection and the Life,' pronounced at the porch.

Thence the long train marched slowly to the City Hall, which was draped in black from ceiling to floor, the drapery being crossed with white bands bearing Mr Parnell's homely death-bed message to his countrymen, 'Give my love to my colleagues and to the Irish people'. The floor was covered with wreaths, the inscription on one running in a somewhat sinister vein. It was a tribute from Mr Parnell's Belfast followers, and bore two mottoes, 'Murdered' and 'Avenge'. Mrs Parnell's three tributes were particularly affecting.

There were two wreaths from Mrs Parnell's daughters, with the words, 'From little Clare and little Kitty to my dear mother's husband'. The coffin rested, appropriately enough, by O'Connell's statue, guarded by Gaelic athletes, while the people passed by it in an apparently endless procession. The funeral cortège proper started from St Stephen's Green for the City Hall, and it contained a notable historic figure in the person of Mr James Stephens, once the head organiser of the 'Irish Republic'. The contingent from Cork bore placards, which they distributed among the crowd, containing the words, 'Murdered to satisfy Englishmen'. The historic side of the event was emphasised by a halt at the spot where Lord Edward Fitzgerald received his death-blow. College Green was one dense mass of men and women, and the most striking scene of all was, perhaps, the passage by the famous old Parliament House, whose glories Mr Parnell had come so near to reviving. The crowd seemed to swell and swell as it neared the beautiful Glasnevin Cemetery, where O'Connell's tomb is, but not his heart which rests at Rome. A correspondent calculates that there were 200,000 persons in all in the procession and in the streets, but it was not swollen by a single anti-Parnellite member or by a priest of the Catholic Church. The sun had set and the moon was up when the coffin reached the turf-lined grave. As it was lowered, tears and sobs burst from the strong men, attached followers of the dead leader, who stood round, and there was bitter weeping while the few parting words were said. There was no disturbance of any kind, nor any outward sign of the bitter feeling which Mr Parnell's death has evoked.

(*Illustrated London News*, 17 October 1891)

Drawing by Philip Mays of the funeral passing the Bank of Ireland where the Irish Parliament assembled in the period before the Act of Union. On two famous occasions Parnell made a theatrical gesture towards the building: in September 1881 after a Land League rally; and in December 1890 following his defeat at Kilkenny. (NLI P&D)

Glasnevin

The funeral passing through Sackville (O'Connell) Street. (*The Graphic*, 17 October 1891)

At the Cemetery

The scene at the cemetery will live in the memory of everyone who had the melancholy privilege of witnessing it. For hours before the time when the head of the funeral procession reached the graveyard vast crowds of people assembled there, and from two o'clock a constant stream of sympathisers passed the gates. The site chosen for the interment is without doubt the very best that could have been selected. It is placed exactly to the left of the mortuary chapel, and at a distance nearly equal to that which divides the chapel from the O'Connell monument and circle. Indeed it is a curiously suggestive fact that the site happens to balance, as it were, from even a picturesque point of view, the place where the Liberator's coffin is laid, and when – as undoubtedly will be the case – a worthy monument is placed over the mound where the chieftain lies, it will form a fitting adjunct to that portion of the graveyard which is properly regarded as the most historically suggestive in the entire ground. It will be known, doubtless, in future as the Parnell Circle, and the recollection of yesterday's extraordinary demonstration of sorrow will for all time mark the place as the centre of sad interest to everyone who may visit the cemetery.

In front of the coffin, upon which lay the old Volunteer flags, walked Mr John O'Connor, MP; Mr T.C. Harrington, MP; Mr H. Harrison, MP; Mr R. Power, MP; Dr Joseph Kenny, MP; Mr John Redmond, MP; Mr William Redmond, MP; Mr Henry Campbell, MP; Mr Edward Harrington, MP; Mr John Clancy, Sub Sheriff; Mr J.L. Carew, MP; Mr J. Wyse Power and others. With them came the Lord Mayor, the High Sheriff and the Corporation officers, the insignia of office being draped in mourning. Miss Dickinson came leaning on the arm of Mr Kerr, the manager of Mr Parnell's property, and she was weeping bitterly. Mrs Dickinson also accompanied them, and with her came Alderman Dillon, Mrs Kenny, and Mr Carew. Miss Katherine Tynan also formed one of the group, and as the coffin was placed beside the grave the scene was inexpressibly touching. Mr Henry Campbell stood at the foot of the grave gazing into it with tears falling fast. Near him stood John and William Redmond, overcome with emotion; and Dr Joseph Kenny, Mr Power, Dr Fitzgerald, Mr Carew, and the other faithful followers of The Chief were bowed down with grief.

(*Weekly Freeman*, 17 October 1891)

The scene in Glasnevin. (*Weekly Freeman*, 17 October 1891)

A family group at the grave the day after the burial: Parnell's sister, Mrs Emily Dickinson, his brother, Henry Tudor Parnell, and one of his nieces, Delia or Alfreda McDermott. (*Evening Press*, 31 March 1958, from a photograph held by St James' Brass and Reed Band)

109

English Views of Parnell

The Illustrated London News *was a weekly magazine which dated from 1842. Its journalists and artists kept the British public informed of events throughout the Empire and over the years Ireland received a good deal of coverage. It was responsible for focussing attention on events such as the Famine, the distress in the west of Ireland in 1879 and the agitation arising from the Plan of Campaign. Generally its treatment of Irish affairs was fair and objective, and its final assessment of Parnell in the issue of 17 October 1891 merits inclusion here.*

Parnell could hold his own with the foremost British politicians of the day who included such formidable figures as Lord Salisbury, Lord Randolph Churchill and Joseph Chamberlain. The one with whom he was most involved was Gladstone. Over the years their relationship changed according to circumstances. During the Land War they were engaged in bitter conflict, but for some years they worked in harmony on the Home Rule issue. Eventually, following the divorce they again became politically opposed. Gladstone's assessment was outlined in an interview which he gave Parnell's biographer, Richard Barry O'Brien, in 1897.

Personal

Mr Parnell, partly on account of the ever-present mystery which surrounded him, is the personality of the hour. The deceased Irish leader's appearance altered greatly at different periods of his life. When the House of Commons first knew him, it was as a handsome man, with lightish brown hair and fine, though cold, grey eyes, a very upright carriage – which he maintained to the end of his life – well-trimmed beard and moustache, and a slight but admirably proportioned figure. A great change was noticeable in the latter half of the 1886 Parliament and up to the date of the divorce case. His dress grew slovenly, and the Irish leader delighted to array himself in Cardigan jackets of strange hue and pattern and rough frieze suits that seemed made in a country tailor's shop. His face put on a waxen and almost livid hue, the eyes grew red and sunken though they retained their strange glitter, the cheeks fell in, and the hair was allowed to fall in thin untidy wisps over the coat collar.

His manners altered with his appearance. A certain social distinction always existed between him and his party, but up to about 1883 the relations were cordial – respectfully admiring on the one hand, easily courteous on the other. Gradually Mr Parnell withdrew himself even from the slight social intercourse in which he had indulged, absented himself from the House for days and even weeks together, refused his address to all and sundry, and

flew into strange fits of passion when it happened to be accidentally disclosed or even hinted at. He kept all power in his hands, nursed the funds carefully – he was also a thorough and methodical man of business and doled out the salaries to the paid members, but exercised only an intermittent control over the policy of his party. There were murmurings and whisperings, but until the great schism they were stifled, as disloyalty to the leader.

Mr Parnell was all his life an ascetic. He ate and drank little, and his only dissipation was the smoking of small, cheap, mild, but evil-smelling cigars. His manners were fine, though so reserved that hardly one of his fellows can recall a single confidence, save, perhaps, during the shock which the Phoenix Park murders caused him. He was the most uncommunicative of men, and he did not always trouble himself to convey correct impressions to journalists and 'interviewers.' Apart from politics, his real interests were in agriculture and chemistry. He was a fair metallurgical chemist himself and loved to dabble in experiments in his laboratory. For books he cared nothing, and he had no culture worth the name.

The late Irish leader had not one of the conventional qualifications of the orator, but few men produced a more remarkable impression on his hearers. The sentences were formless and often ungrammatical, the speaker seeming too indifferent to trouble about rounding them off. He would pause to catch up the thread of his discourse, get confused with his notes and figures, and often mistake arguments and statistics. Yet, at his best, he gave an idea of personal force which was irresistible. He was then extremely clear and pointed, and his striking appearance, his voice, with a certain ring of quiet scorn in it corresponding to the masterful set of his face, secured for him a more intent audience even than Mr Gladstone was always able to attract. In such moments he was an orator in spite of himself, a bizarre and significant figure, of whom even the House of Commons stood – in his later years at least – in some degree of awe.

(*Illustrated London News*, 17 October 1891)

An Appreciation

Richard Barry O'Brien: 'Could you say what it was that first attracted your attention to Parnell?'

Mr Gladstone (with much energy): 'Parnell was the most remarkable man I ever met. I do not say the ablest man; I say the most remarkable and the most interesting. He was an intellectual phenomenon. He was unlike anyone I had ever met. He did things and he said things unlike other men. His ascendency over his party was extraordinary. There has never been anything like it in my experience in the House of Commons. He succeeded in surrounding himself with very clever men, with men exactly suited for his purpose. They have changed since, I don't know why. Everything seems to have changed. But in his time he had a most efficient party, an extraordinary party. I do not say extraordinary as an Opposition, but extraordinary as a Government. The absolute obedience, the strict discipline, the military discipline, in which he held them was unlike anything I have ever seen'.

'May I ask, when did you first speak to Parnell?'

Mr Gladstone: 'Well, under very peculiar circumstances, and they illustrate what I mean when I speak of him being unlike anyone I ever met. I was in the House of Commons, and it was in 1881, when, you know, we were at war. Parnell had made violent speeches in Ireland. He had stirred the people up to lawlessness. Forster had

those speeches printed. He put them into my hands. I read them carefully. They made a deep impression on me, and I came down to the House and attacked Parnell. I think I made rather a strong speech' (with a smile) – 'drew up rather a strong indictment against him, for some of the extracts were very bad. Well, he sat still all the time, was quite immovable. He never interrupted me; he never even made a gesture of dissent. I remember there was one declaration of his which was outrageous in its lawlessness. I read it slowly and deliberately, and watched him the while. He never winced, while the House was much moved. He listened attentively, courteously, but showed no feeling, no excitement, no concern. I sat down. He did not rise to reply. He looked as if he were the one individual in the House who was not a bit affected by what I said. The debate went on. After a time I walked out of the House. He rose from his seat, followed me, and coming up with much dignity and in a very friendly way, said: "Mr Gladstone, I should like to see those extracts from my speeches which you read. I should like particularly to see that last declaration. Would you allow me to see your copy?" I said, "Certainly," and I returned to the table, got the copy, and brought it back to him. He glanced through it quickly. Fastening at once on the most violent declaration, he said, very quietly: "That's wrong; I never used those words. The report is quite wrong. I am much obliged to you for letting me see it." And, sir' (with vehemence), 'he was right. The report was wrong. The Irish Government had blundered. But Parnell went away quite unconcerned. He did not ask me to look into the matter. He was apparently wholly indifferent. Of course I did look into the matter, and made it right. But Parnell, to all appearances, did not care. That was my first interview with him, and it made a deep impression on me. The immobility of the man, the laconic way of dealing with the subject, his utter indifference to the opinion of the House – the whole thing was so extraordinary and so unlike what one was accustomed to in such circumstances.'

(R.B. O'Brien, *Parnell*, ii, 357-9)

Recollections of Colleagues

Justin McCarthy and T.P. O'Connor were friends and associates of Parnell for many years. Although they opposed him at the end, they went to great lengths to find a compromise acceptable to him. Michael Davitt was close to Parnell in the late 1870s and was responsible for initiating the land agitation which brought him to national prominence. However, their views diverged from an early stage and after the divorce Davitt was one of his most outspoken critics.

Apart from their involvement in politics, all three worked as journalists and were experienced judges of personality and character.

Charles Stewart Parnell

Anyhow, Parnell and I were near neighbours for a considerable time; and he used to come often from his 'squalid lodging' in Keppel Street to visit me in my 'squalid' Gower Street home. We had some pleasant dinner-parties in that home now and then; and I remember that it was there Parnell first made the personal acquaintance of Sir Charles Gavan Duffy, of Mr Leonard Courtney, and of Charles Russell, as he was then, at present Lord Russell of Killowen. Parnell used to come to see me often quite informally in the early afternoons, and the casual visits always had to be early because we both had to attend the sittings of the House of Commons, he as a Member of the House, and I as a writer of leading articles for the *Daily News*. I am speaking of the days before I myself found a place on the green benches of the House. Parnell soon became a great favourite with all the members of my family, and his presence was always welcome. He was then a handsome man, still quite young, with a tall and stately figure, and a singularly sweet and winning smile. He had the easy manners of a perfect gentleman. Two members of my family were very young persons when we first came to know Parnell, and he delighted them by his sympathetic ways and by the genial ease with which he made himself interested in their occupations. I have never met in my life a better-bred man than Parnell.

I have lately read a great deal about his chilling manners, about his haughty superciliousness, about his positive rudeness to strangers and, indeed, to all persons whom he considered in any way beneath himself, so far as social position was concerned. I can only say that, if the man thus described was Parnell, then I never knew Parnell at all, never could even have seen him. For the Parnell with whom I was in closest intimacy for some fifteen years bore not the slightest resemblance to that other Parnell, but was indeed in every way curiously unlike him.

I have seen him in all sorts of companionships, tried by all manner of provocations, beset by bores, perplexed by worries, and I never saw in his manner anything that did not belong to the character of a thorough gentleman. I have read over and over again about some lowly-born member of Parnell's party having so far forgotten his humble station as to address his leader by the name of 'Parnell,' and being instantly rebuked by frowning brow and chilling tone, and the words 'Mr Parnell, if you please.' Now, of course, it is not possible for me to say that no such incident ever occurred, because I could not profess to have been present at every interchange of words between Parnell and any other member, or all the members of his party. I can only say that the whole story seems to me to tell of something utterly unlike any way or characteristic of Parnell's which ever came under my observation.

(J. McCarthy, *Reminiscences,* ii, 90-92)

Parnell: Characteristics and Estimate

First as to Mr Parnell's appearance. As he was, so he looked. The iron resolution, the impenetrable reserve, the frigid fanaticism were written in his lithe figure, and still more in the strange, striking, unique countenance. Before ill-health lined and hollowed it, his face was one of the handsomest in the House of Commons. The nose was long, large, straight, well-chiselled; the mouth was small and well-carved, but mobile with pride, passion, and scorn; the voice was clear, sure, and penetrating and, when he was excited, could be thrilling, so that sometimes you could imagine that it had a power to control, and even terrorise, the House of Commons; his forehead was beautiful, – perfectly round, white, and lofty. But, after all, in looking at him, as in the case of every remarkable man, the eyes were the most striking feature. They were the most meaning eyes I have ever seen. They were of the hard dark sort, which you see in the Red Indian – red-brown, like flint; but who can describe their varying lights and expressions? Sometimes you thought they never changed, for they certainly never revealed anything; at others, they seemed to flash and burn; and they always had a strange glow in them that arrested your attention. It was this latent expression that suggested to so many people the impression that his end would be tragic. I once heard a poet declare that with such a face and air, Mr Parnell was foredoomed to the scaffold. The reality has proved almost worse than such forecasts, for he has died prematurely and sorrowfully amid the hideous discord of faction, where once he had stood on an eminence as unquestioned as ever a human leader enjoyed.

He was always a very simple eater, and never seemed to care for creature comforts in any shape. He was not a man to accept death submissively. Combative, unimaginative, obstinate, he would fight for life with the same unconquerable tenacity with which he would defend anything else which he believed to be his right, and accordingly he made a desperate struggle for years against the advance of disease. He used to eat rather heartily – though only twice a day; but he drank sparingly, and usually only the thinnest of claret and Rhine wine. Indeed, in many ways he was a natural ascetic. But he was told by his doctor that he ate unwisely the wrong things at the wrong time; and he was put on a strict regime which he faithfully carried out. He usually sat at the same table; and in the old days of a united party there were three or four colleagues who always shared the repast. There, the waiter would bring in carefully-toasted brown bread, a small fried sole, and a bird, with a pint of Moselle wine, to which dinner he rigidly adhered.

T.P. O'Connor, *Parnell*, pp. 213-5)

Death of Parnell: Appreciation

Magnanimity or gratitude he had none. His mind had few if any generous impulses, and was barren of all faith except a boundless belief in himself. Here, he possessed the fanaticism of the zealot, and made a fatalistic confidence in his own destiny the dominating idea of his political career. He frequently quoted two lines of Shakespeare which inculcated fidelity to one's self as the rule of existence. Herein, lay the secret of his pride and the vulnerable spot in Achilles's heel. A fanatical cult of one's own ego in a public man beset by temptations, untempered by a little human heresy borrowed from the wisdom of the serpent, if not from any higher moral source, is very apt to beget infidelity to the nobler duties and obligations of life, and thereby to injure or to isolate the idol of self-worship.

These faults in the human portraiture of Parnell are but like the wart on Cromwell's face. They not only do not conceal his greatness, they attest it by a testimony which would damn smaller men to the level of comparative mediocrity. He has left the impress of his personality and power in the work he has done, and in the universal recognition that exists of the part he has played in the drama of Ireland's struggle against one of the greatest of the world's empires. His fame is a national asset for Ireland, and if the lives and labours of her great men are to be guides and incentives to those who are to maintain the fight for Irish liberty, the faults as well as the virtues of the Wolfe Tones, O'Connells, Butts, Stephenses, and Parnells must be looked at, in charity, it is true, but as truth all the same.

(M. Davitt, *Fall of Feudalism*, p. 658)

John Howard Recalls

Parnell's elder brother, John Howard, knew him all his life and apart, perhaps, from Katharine O'Shea, understood him better than anybody else. His book is full of revealing insights, some of which have already been quoted.

Parnell had a keen sense of humour and some of his eccentricities may have been calculated. His dread of funerals, however, was real and may have originated when, at the age of thirteen, he was the only member of the family present at his father's funeral. Death was never far distant from him: in his short lifetime he also lost a daughter, three sisters, a brother and a nephew; in addition his brother William had died before he was born.

Charley's Superstitions

I did not notice any particular instances of superstition in Charley during his childhood and boyhood. But in later life a tendency to ascribe an omen for good or ill to the most trivial occurrence, and to see the finger of Fate in the most commonplace objects, became very noticeable. I think it was after the railway accident in America that Charley first began to develop this curious trait in his character.

One of his most remarkable superstitions was his aversion to the colour green, although it was the national colour of Ireland. Accordingly, he never wore a coat or tie that had the slightest tinge of green in its material and, as I mention elsewhere, steadily refused to wear the fine green travelling-rug which was presented to him. He carried to strange limits this dislike of the colour green in any shape or form. Once he wrote home to one of his sisters – I believe Mrs Dickinson – who had told me that she had just had his room at Avondale re-papered, saying: 'I hope you have not had my room done in green, as, if so, I shall never use it.'

Funerals always caused him intense dread and he never could be persuaded to attend one, even when the deceased happened to be one of his most intimate friends.

The number thirteen, of course, was always an unlucky one, in his opinion. He steadily refused, even at the risk of annoying or offending his host, to sit down thirteen at table. On one occasion he had put up at a country hotel during election time, and had gone up to his room to prepare himself for dinner. The friend who was travelling with him, and who occupied a room next to Charley's was surprised a moment or so later to hear a knock on his door, and to find, when he opened it, Charley standing in the passage with his bag looking very much upset. The friend asked what was the matter, and he replied by pointing to the number on his door, which was 13, and remarking: 'What a room to give me! I suppose the landlord is a Tory, and has done this on purpose.'

The Wink of the Sphinx

... As he gradually grew out of childhood, this reserve of Charley's became more and more accentuated. The greater portion of it was undoubtedly due to a mixture of nervousness and pride, resulting in a sort of shy repulsion towards allowing his inner thoughts and real nature to appear on the surface, to be at the mercy of the multitude. There was also, it must be owned, at times what appeared to be just a trace of affectation in this Sphinx-like attitude towards the world in general. ...

I remember meeting Charley, when he was in the height of his glory, one day in Kildare Street. I had only just returned from one of my trips to America, and had that morning seen him at Morrison's Hotel. I was expecting to meet him at Harcourt Street Station in the evening and to go down with him to Avondale. We were going in opposite directions and passed on the same pavement, almost touching one another. Charley, however, showed not the slightest sign of recognition until we were almost side by side; then he just winked the eye nearest to me.

It was no sign of boisterous jollity or facetious slyness, such as the dropping of the eyelid generally betokens. Charley simply wished to show that he had seen and recognised me, but did not wish to disturb his demeanour of perfect composure and aloofness. And how great an asset that aloofness was perhaps he himself only knew. It was not only an armour against the English; it was a robe that attracted the loyalty, and even the wild enthusiasm, of his own countrymen, while at the same time repelling their intimacy.

So it can easily be understood that Charley's mind could not be read as a book. It was only a stray straw that gave an indication – often not more than a suspicion – of the way the wind was blowing.

(J.H. Parnell, *Parnell*, pp. 126-7, 263-5)

(*The Parnell Commission*, p.4)

There he is: the brother. Image of him. Haunting face. Now that's a coincidence. Course hundreds of times you think of a person and don't meet him. Like a man walking in his sleep. No-one knows him. Must be a corporation meeting today. They say he never put on the city marshal's uniform since he got the job. Charley Boulger used to come out on his high horse, cocked hat, puffed, powdered and shaved. Look at the woebegone walk of him. Eaten a bad egg. Poached eyes on ghost. I have a pain. Great man's brother: his brother's brother. He'd look nice on the city charger. Drop into the D.B.C. probably for his coffee, play chess there. His brother used men as pawns. Let them all go to pot. Afraid to pass a remark on him. Freeze them up with that eye of his. That's the fascination: the name. All a bit touched. Mad Fanny and his other sister Mrs Dickinson driving about with scarlet harness. Bolt upright like surgeon M'Ardle. Still David Sheehy beat him for south Meath. Apply for the Chiltern Hundreds and retire into public life. The patriot's banquet. Eating orangepeels in the park. Simon Dedalus said when they put him in parliament that Parnell would come back from the grave and lead him out of the House of Commons by the arm.

(James Joyce, *Ulysses*, p. 168)

– John Howard was appointed to the ceremonial post of City Marshal by Dublin Corporation around 1898. From 1895 to 1900 he was the Irish Party (Redmondite) MP for South Meath. In 1903 he contested the constituency as an independent but was defeated by the official candidate, David Sheehy.

Celebration

NO. 1 (NEW SERIES) JANUARY 1937.

A BROADSIDE

EDITORS: DOROTHY WELLESLEY AND W. B. YEATS.
PUBLISHED MONTHLY AT THE CUALA PRESS, ONE HUNDRED
AND THIRTY THREE LOWER BAGGOT STREET, DUBLIN.

COME GATHER ROUND ME PARNELLITES

Come gather round me Parnellites
And praise our chosen man;
Stand upright on your legs awhile;
Stand upright while you can
For soon we lie where he is laid
And he is underground.
Come fill up all those glasses
And pass the bottle round.

And here's a cogent reason,
And I have many more,
He fought the might of England
And saved the Irish poor;
Whatever good a farmer's got
He brought it all to pass;
And here's another reason,
That Parnell loved a lass.

And here's a final reason,
He was of such a kind
Every man that sings a song
Keeps Parnell in his mind,
For Parnell was a proud man,
No prouder trod the ground,
And a proud man's a lovely man
So pass the bottle round.

The Bishops and the Party
That tragic story made.
A husband who had sold his wife
And after that betrayed;
But stories that live longest
Are sung above a glass;
And Parnell loved his country,
And Parnell loved a lass.

W. B. Yeats.

A Cuala Press broadside with woodcut by Jack B. Yeats and poem by W.B. Yeats, 1937.

The Blackbird of Avondale;
Or, the Arrest of
PARNELL.

By the sweet bay of Dublin whilst carelessly strolling,
   I sat myself down by a green myrtle shade,
Reclined on the beach as the wild waves were rolling,
   In sorrow condoling I saw a fair maid ;
Her robes changed to mourning that once shone so glorious
   I stood in amazement to hear her sad wail,
Her heart-strings burst out in wild accents uproarious,
   Oh, where is my Blackbird of sweet Avondale.

Section of a broadside ballad. (NLI)

One morning you would open the paper, the cabman affirmed, and read, *Return of Parnell*. He bet them what they liked. A Dublin fusilier was in that shelter one night and said he saw him in South Africa. Pride it was killed him. He ought to have done away with himself or lain low for a time after Committee Room No. 15 until he was his old self again with no-one to point a finger at him. Then they would all to a man have gone down on their marrowbones to him to come back when he had recovered his senses. Dead he wasn't. Simply absconded somewhere. The coffin they brought over was full of stones. He changed his name to De Wet, the Boer general. He made a mistake to fight the priests. And so forth and so on.
(James Joyce, *Ulysses,* p. 645)

Index